THE COLLECTED POEMS OF
LEW SARETT

LEW SARETT

From a recent photograph by J. D. Toloff, F.R.P.S.

THE
COLLECTED
POEMS OF
LEW SARETT

WITH A FOREWORD BY
CARL SANDBURG

NEW YORK
HENRY HOLT AND COMPANY

MANY, MANY MOONS

COPYRIGHT, 1920,
BY HENRY HOLT AND COMPANY

THE BOX OF GOD

COPYRIGHT, 1922,
BY HENRY HOLT AND COMPANY

SLOW SMOKE

COPYRIGHT, 1925,
BY HENRY HOLT AND COMPANY

WINGS AGAINST THE MOON

COPYRIGHT, 1931,
BY HENRY HOLT AND COMPANY, INC.

COLLECTED POEMS

COPYRIGHT, 1941,
BY HENRY HOLT AND COMPANY, INC.

First Printing

CONTENTS

v

II

THE BOX OF GOD

III

TRAILING ARBUTUS

for

M. H. S.

IV

TAMARACK BLUE

V

SPLIT-RAIL FENCES

VI

FLYING MOCCASINS

vii

VII

THREE WOMEN

VIII

SADDLE-LEATHER

IX

COUNCIL-FIRES

X

TINDER AND FLINT

XI

FIGURES IN BRONZE

XII

RED GODS

XIII

LUMBERJACKS AND VOYAGEURS

FOREWORD

Books say Yes to life. Or they say No. "The Collected Poems of Lew Sarett" says Yes.

Picking classics in contemporary books is like picking winners in baseball or durable forms of government among nations. One man's guess is as good as another's.

We might say, "Herewith is entered Lew Sarett and his 'Collected Poems' as a runner for a place among the classics." And it would be only a guess.

However, there is nothing in the stipulations of the Espionage Act nor in the Code of Chesterfield nor in the Marquis of Queensbury rules, that stops us from asking:

"Why not the loam and the lingo, the sand and the syllables of North America in the books of North America?"

And so Sarett . . . with tall timbers, fresh waters, blue ducks, and a loon in him. The loon, a poet's bird for sure, is here. Unless there is a loon cry in a book the poetry is gone out of it. We have too many orderly, respectable, synthesized poets in the United States and in England. In their orientation with the library canary fed from delicatessen tins, they are strangers to the loon that calls off its long night cry in tall timber up among the beginnings of the Mississippi.

Lew Sarett has equipment. Years a forest ranger and a woodsman, other years a wilderness guide, companion of red and white men as an outrider of civilization, university professor, headline performer on the American platform, magazine writer, he brings wisdom of things silent and things garrulous to his book. Old men with strong heads and shrewd slow tongues, young men with tough feet, the wishing song of mate for mate—they are here. The loam and the lingo, the sand and the syllables of North America are here "The Collected Poems of Lew Sarett" says Yes.

CARL SANDBURG.

INTRODUCTION

The roots of America strike deep into a rich earth, into the soil of a vast and varied wilderness. It was once, and in many respects is still, a dramatic expanse of brooding mountains and forests, of fertile Southern river-bottoms and stony New England hills, of plains and seas whose horizons challenge the imagination.

Men are shaped much by the soil on which they live, by the latitude, the formation, and the fertility of the region that sustains them. Their lives are affected profoundly by their environment of rivers and forests, by prevailing floods and drouths, by wind and weather—by nature. The character of the American draws its color and strength largely from the wild earth of America. It is no accident that the dominant traits of the American are his independence, his individualism, his forthrightness, his rebellion against restraints, and his passion for freedom. These are in part the effects of definite causes that lie in the character of our land.

Inevitably, therefore, the story of our country is largely an heroic tale of the soil and of the folk who derive their vitality from the earth. It is a thrilling record of the ventures of fur-traders and voyageurs, of cowpunchers and prospectors, of farmers and railway builders and loggers, who hurled themselves at the gigantic barriers of mountains and deserts and forests; of pioneers who fought toe to toe with every form of adversity which nature can devise; who finally subdued a stubborn land and established an amazing nation.

Many of us in this nation are moved deeply by that drama of the frontiers, by the past and present glory of rural America. We are interested in the brute and human creatures who have played—and are playing—roles in that epical conquest, in the buffalo, the bear, and the coyote, in the cowhand, the ranger, and the farmer, in the lumberjack, the French-Canadian coureur de bois, and the Indian.

No doubt some Americans, urban and sophisticated, regard these rural regions and folk as remote in time and in geography—and of no great consequence. How amusing an attitude like this, when one considers that the United States is overwhelmingly agrarian in its expanse and in the source of its strength. Others of us, however, feel that these regions and their earthy folk are of great moment: they represent a precious inheritance; the remnants of them are a vital part of the life of our country today; they give America much of her peculiar identity, color, and power; and they are in the blood of America. Indeed, some of us think that these are all that matter much—the wild earth, nature: the enduring mountains that look down imperturbably on the human race, on its troubles, its momentary triumphs, its passing vanities; the permanent, fecund earth which yields up its fruit century on century and sustains the brute and human life of the world. We love the solid companionship of the simple folk of the soil, who, unlike their clever, urban brothers, are candid, predictable, and robust of spirit; who are sturdy and wear well; who are producers and not parasites in our economic life; who are energizers and not devitalizers in the blood-stream of America. And a few of us are convinced that nature holds most of the answers to the big basic questions of life, that nature holds much of whatever in life is touched with joy, meaning, and beauty.

Feeling thus deeply, we devote our lives to these matters. Some of us dedicate ourselves in our vocations and our recreations to forest life or to the sea, to gardening or to farm life, to exploring woods and waters, or to discovering the rich resources of the wilderness. Others of us commit ourselves to scientific research into the ways of nature in order to unravel her mysteries and to tap the unplumbed reservoirs of power within her. And a few of us set out to devote our lives to re-creating for others the beauty of wild America; to writing much and to speaking much of American backwoods and frontiers, of wolves and deer and bear, of loggers and voyageurs and Indians.

Hence this collection of poems. It is the outgrowth of many years of life on the vanishing frontiers of the Rocky Mountains and of the forests of the Lake Superior region. It is an expression—however inadequate—of the feeling that much of whatever is joyous and significant in life, timeless, true, and peculiarly American, tends to be rooted in the wild earth of America.

Moving in and out of the old and new frontiers is one bronze figure not clearly understood by many of us—the American Indian. In certain groups of poems in this collection I have tried to capture the essence of this primitive American, especially the poetry implicit in his character, his life, and his modes of expression, in his songs, his dances, and his ceremonies, in his council-oratory, his legends, and his religion. In many other groups I have sought to capture the poetry in some of the white characters of our remote borderlands, in mountaineers, plainsmen, and woodsmen, and in the wild creatures of our wilderness. These latter borderland folk are somewhat familiar types to most readers. One may write of white frontiersmen and wild animals with the confidence that the reader will bring to one's writings a more or less adequate background of information concerning their places in the American scene and their ways of life. Therefore, the groups of poems which deal with the mountains of the West and the forests of the North, with the white backwoods folk and wild creatures who move through them, make no uncommon demands on the reader; they require no special pleading. One does not need to supplement them with an Appendix or an Introduction. The fact that I shall not discuss in these supplementary sections the many poems on white pioneers, on wild animals, and on nature does not imply a lack of concern with them. On the contrary, backwoods folk, wild creatures, and nature concern me profoundly. They explain in part the Indian who walks through many of the pages of this book: they are an integral part of his life; they are his antagonists and his protagonists; they shape his character. More than this, these white characters and wild creatures are important in their own right: they are bound up with the spectacular past of our nation and to a large extent with its virile present; they lie at the core of our history; they are intensely American characters in an intensely American scene. But they are closer to the currents of our lives than is the Indian. The poems of the frontier and nature, therefore, demand no out of the ordinary background; they may stand on their own legs. But a few of the Indian pieces—not all, by any means—require supplementary information. Hence this explanatory Introduction and the subsequent Appendix. I offer them with the thought that these—with the poems on which they bear—may enable the reader to grasp more readily the nature of the red man and of his life as they are treated in this book.

It is impossible, of course, to tell the whole story of the Original American in a collection of poems, an Introduction and a brief Appendix. It is possible, however, in this limited space to provide technical information on Indian practices and beliefs which may throw light on some of the poems and may help to build a somewhat better understanding of the Indian, and especially of the poetry in him—my chief concern in the Indian studies.

In many respects the red man is a personality and symbol peculiarly American. He plays a role in nearly every tale of American frontiers. He is bound up with our traditions. He warrants attention for what he is even today: for the complex social and economic problem created by the three hundred sixty thousand Indians in the United States; and for the real contribution the Indian is making to our arts. Assuredly, we should strive to understand this Original American and to preserve in our traditions the aboriginal color, character, and culture which are rapidly vanishing under the pressure of white civilization. Indeed, we must understand him if we are to understand our own origin as a nation.

Yet the average American gives little thought to the Indian of the past fifty years. He regards him as a remote creature, monosyllabic, sullen, unfathomable. He may picture him romantically: the circus type of Indian dressed in buckskin and eagle plumes, dangling at his waist bloody scalps, with upraised battle-ax stalking his white enemies in the forest—a picture that might have been true of an occasional Indian of a century ago. Or, somewhat familiar with the modern red man, he may imagine him with stark realism as struggling desperately for survival on his reservations, the dupe of cunning white men, ravaged by tuberculosis and trachoma, tattered, famished, frustrated, eking out a gaunt living by scratching the earth for a few potatoes or a handful of corn. Obviously, both pictures are extreme. The Indian is neither of these types—and he is both. He is at once crass and beautiful, mercenary and idealistic, amusing and tragic. But at all times he is full of the stuff of poetry.

Although the life of the North American Indian shines with the gold of poetry, he has no definite form of expression called "poetry." His poetry is implicit in his songs, in his dances, in his religion, and in his mode of expressing himself in council-talks, invocations, and ceremonies. The specific words which he utters in a song may be few. A literal interpretation of the words of a song or ritual, therefore, will rarely reveal the freight of ideas and beauty in the song or ceremony. For example, the only words expressed in a meaningful Chippewa war-dance may be the following:

> I am dancing in the sky,
> I am dancing in the sky
> With the scalp of a Cut-throat.

But the few words may imply much. In his songs and dances the Indian habitually suggests his ideas rather than states them explicitly. The few words uttered usually represent the peak of an emotional or an imaginative flight. If these words are supplemented by an understanding of the accompanying ritual, symbols, dance steps, and pantomime, and by knowledge of Indian legends, superstitions, and reli-

xx

gion, the fragmentary phrases of the song may suggest a wealth of ideas and beauty.

The Indian themes in Parts VI, Flying Moccasins, and XII, Red Gods, are therefore in no sense literal interpretations of aboriginal songs, dances, and rituals. They are not even approximate interpretations. They are original poems. They are based on typical, fragmentary Indian utterances in Indian ceremonies, which I strive to interpret and amplify in the light of aboriginal beliefs and practices. They are efforts to dramatize more explicitly in the English language ideas and feelings merely suggested by Indian originals.

In his council-oratory, however, the Indian is more prodigal of language, more explicit, and more didactic. Consequently, the council-talk poems in Part IX, Council-Fires, though still not translations, are closer to definite originals. Most of them are based on council-talks I have heard among the Chippewas. In these pieces I have tried faithfully to reproduce genuine Indian speech-situations and common Indian problems and issues; I have tried to capture faithfully Indian habits of thought and feeling and to translate them into genuine Indian idiom.

The Indian narratives and character studies in Parts II, The Box of God, IV, Tamarack Blue, VII, Three Women, and XI, Figures in Bronze, are obviously in no respect translations or even interpretations. They are more or less objective studies of typical red men and of poignant situations in their primitive life.

In all the Indian poems in this book, however, I have tried to be faithful to the fundamental nature of the aboriginal American, and to preserve as accurately as possible his legends and traditions, his outlook on life and on the universe, and his peculiar ways of expressing himself.

I have sought, moreover, to maintain consistently the point of view of the Indian of the past fifty years and of today, and not that of the romanticized red man of a century ago. I am concerned chiefly with the modern reservation Indian, in his transition from primitive wild life to the white man's civilization. I have tried to reveal the innumerable paradoxes of his life in the past few decades, with its strange marriage of the old and the new, of the bizarre and the beautiful, of paganism and Christianity, of the banal and the sublime.

The red man in his picturesque setting of teepees and travois, of thundering buffalos and ambushed prairie-schooners heaped with scalped dead, has gone the way of the flintlock. With this colorful savage has vanished much of the romance of our wild yesterdays. Yet in the life of the Indian of the past half century there is a beauty that is often more moving, and certainly more kaleidoscopic, than that of the old days of the war-dance. In this transitional type of Indian living on the modern reservation there is a rugged, earthy quality that is distinctive of the New World. About this bronze figure, the symbol of our vanishing West, hovers an atmosphere as American as the fragrance of burning pine.

Beneath the often drab surface of the modern red man, there is an abundance of the crude ore of poetry. The ingredients of poetry are in his characteristic imagery, in his idiom, and in the mysticism that marks his religion. Power lies in the aboriginal rhythms that move him to pound his feet on the ground and to shout heavenward in the war-songs, ceremonies, and medicine-dances which he still preserves. Wistful beauty marks the minor melodies of the love songs which he plays on his cedar flute. His council-oratory is more than interesting in its mingling of banality and grandeur, of simplicity of utterance and sonorous rhetoric, of the mundane and the idealistic. His life is full of the rough elements of drama, of comedy, and of tragedy. Consider his desperate struggle of the past century to stem the tide of a bewildering, inexorable civilization whose inconsistencies he could not always grasp; to withstand the ravages of the white man's diseases to which he has not yet built up an immunity; to beat off the astute white swindlers who were ever ready to pounce upon him as wolves upon a wounded deer. In the drama enacted in our American wilderness he has played every role: hero and villain, hunter and hunted, victor and vanquished. Yesterday, defiant, imperious in his manner, gallantly he fought for his life with naked hands against storm and snow, against flood and fury, against man and beast and pestilence; heroically he fastened his fingers on the throat of a hostile world and forced it to yield up a living for himself, for his family, and for his tribe. Today, poverty-stricken, more or less broken, stripped of much of his former high color and grandeur, he is making his exit in the West and the North, fading in the dusk and darkness of oblivion.

And oblivion it is, in the opinion of many of us, notwithstanding the apparent increase in the Indian population of the United States in the past fifty years. Some of us feel that the numerical increase is misleading, for it represents additional mixed-bloods—the result of the infusion of white blood. The number of full-blooded pagan Indians, of Indians of pure racial type, in many tribes—not all—is steadily decreasing.

In all this time and trouble, when the red man was driven

from pillar to post, he had but one powerful friend, except for the occasional white missionary: the United States Bureau of Indian Affairs in the Department of the Interior. And even this agency for good often gave a sorry account of its guardianship. It is only in recent years that the Office of Indian Affairs has attacked the Indian problem consistently with intelligence, sympathy, and vision.

Again, consider the dramatic religious struggle which still goes on in the hearts of many of the older Indians today as they strive naively to reconcile in their lives two irreconcilable religions, Christianity and paganism; to follow concurrently monotheism and animism. My mind goes back to Alex Down-wind, who rang the church bell zealously on Sunday morning and worshiped God devoutly in the little Christian mission on the pine-clad bluffs overlooking Lake Superior, but who on Sunday night retired furtively to the dark woods two miles from the Indian village to his medicine-lodge to conjure the evil spirits to his side. I can still see him in the firelight, chanting, beating his drum, invoking the evil spirits to help him make potent medicine for the assembled Indians—for a consideration: medicine to paralyze the limbs of an enemy; medicine to enable a young man to seduce a loved one; medicine to enable a woman to commune with the spirit of her dead husband. Can these religions be reconciled? An old Indian can reconcile them—somehow.

The musical expression of the aboriginal American, however cacophonous to white ears, contains poetry. The starkly elemental, and sometimes profoundly stylized, dances, in which the pagan elder folk—and many of the young—for a moment dance their way out of their rags and realism back to the splendor of another day, or into the lofty realm of the spirit which many Indians attain even today—these hold moments of power and beauty.

Dignity, economy of word, vivid imagery, and irony distinguish his council-speaking. His deliberative speeches sometimes rise to great heights.

Imagination and fervor color his rituals and his religion. His animistic interpretations of the phenomena of nature are complex and complete in their personification of earth and sky and water, of beast and bird and reptile, of the flash of lightning, the rumble of thunder, and the roar of big winds. Indian metaphysics may strike the white man as preposterous; nevertheless, the red man's interpretation of the universe and of man's place in it is on the whole big, sweeping, and bold in its scope and contours, and certainly to the minds of the older Indians it is more real, immediate, and compelling than the white man's explanation of life. Mysticism and a dreadful reality and imminence mark the supernatural world in which the so-called pagan Indian lives. He walks through life every day, every hour, communing with the spirits that reside in pine and eagle and star, ever invoking the ghosts of the evil and the ghosts of the good who crowd the dark universe. We smile patronizingly at some of his elemental notions, but the Indian possessed a religion that was terribly real to him; and he really worked at his religion—seven days of the week.

The life of the aboriginal American is not wholly somber; it has its high lights of humor and comedy. Grotesquery crops up in some of his attempts to adapt himself to the white man's mode of living with its baffling machines and its incomprehensible customs. Incongruity often marks his culture—even the furnishings of his wigwam or cabin, with its agglomeration of beaded buckskin medicine-bags and alarm clocks, of papoose cradle-boards and cosmetic jars, of stone pestles and mortars and battered phonographs. I am reminded of the old Chippewa buck who was given by the government title in fee simple to a tract of one hundred sixty acres of choice Minnesota pine, which was to be his home thereafter. He traded his valuable homestead—all that he possessed in the world—to a conscienceless white man for a team of black horses with glittering silver harness and a shining black hearse with plate glass windows and blowing black plumes. Proudly he drove the horses hitched to the hearse back to the Chippewa village in order to impress his neighbors. And within the hearse, behind the glass windows, in place of a coffin, squatted his ample squaw beaming and bowing right and left. The incident was amusing? Yes—and tragic. It illustrates a trait too common in Indians once upon a time. But there are few Indians as gullible and childlike as these Indians nowadays. The red man has learned his lessons in the school of bitter experience.

One finds much of interest in the dialectic novelty of his speech. The pidgin-English of the woods Indians on the Canadian border is an odd hybrid language in which the simple beauty of original Indian idiom is now shot through with twisted frontier slang and French-Canadian patois.

The drollness and comedy of the Indian of the past half century—rooted largely in anachronism and paradox—is epitomized perhaps by the incongruous costume he sometimes wears in impressive ceremonial dances: a nondescript outfit of beaded buckskin moccasins and the woolen underdrawers of the white man, a gaudy satin shirt and eagle plumes, sleigh-bells at his ankles or knees and a beaded medicine-bag in his hands.

Indeed, most of what is amusing, poignant, and tragic in the red man of the past few decades grows out of the unresolved clash of two civilizations in him, of two opposed cultures. In a few more years the conflict will be resolved. One civilization, one culture, will dominate the red man. It will be the white man's. The Indian, as a pure racial type and as a spectacular aboriginal figure, will be merged with the white American in mind and heart, in ritual and daily routine. He will exist only in the traditions of America as a dramatic personality, as an arresting American character of our heroic past.

It is the poetry of this relatively modern but vanishing type of reservation Indian which I wish to preserve in the Indian themes in Parts II, IV, VI, VII, IX, and XII of this book. In the remaining groups—and these constitute the bulk of this volume—I have tried to capture the spirit of the Indian's—and white man's—background of wild nature and of the creatures, four-footed and two-footed, who dwell in the backwoods and borderlands of our country.

Despite a persistent effort to record these matters objectively, it may be that one's report is colored by one's feelings and by what one is as a human being. In narrating facts it is difficult to avoid betraying one's human reactions to the facts —even if it were desirable. What a man is necessarily colors every line of what he writes. Therefore, in a book of this character one inevitably writes oneself down collaterally as a human being, for good or for ill.

In any event, I have written this collection of poems on the mountains, the deserts, and the forests of America, and on the brute and human folk who range its wilderness, because I feel that these aspects of American life should contain for Americans some degree of meaning. I have written about these simple folk of the earth, moreover, because I have lived with them, I know them, I find pleasure in their companionship, and my spirit belongs to them. Lastly, I have written about them because it gives me joy to write about them.

If this collection of poems, therefore, conveys to others a slight measure of the wild beauty of America, of her mountain ways and forest life, and if in some degree it gives others pleasure, I shall be glad. If it does not thus succeed—it was Walter Savage Landor who said, "There is delight in singing, though none hear beside the singer."

LEW SARETT.

PART I

TOOTH AND CLAW

TO A WILD GOOSE OVER DECOYS

O lonely trumpeter, coasting down the sky,
Like a winter leaf blown from the bur-oak tree
By whipping winds, and flapping silverly
Against the sun—I know your lonely cry.

I know the worn wild heart that bends your flight
And circles you above this beckoning lake,
Eager of neck, to find the honking drake
Who speaks of reedy refuge for the night.

I know the sudden rapture that you fling
In answer to our friendly gander's call—
Halloo! Beware decoys!—or you will fall
With a silver bullet whistling in your wing!

Beat on your weary flight across the blue!
Beware, O traveller, of our gabbling geese!
Beware this weedy counterfeit of peace! . . .
Oh, I was once a passing bird like you.

GRANITE

O stolid granite hills, that tower serene
Above the world, its high concerns and mean,
Stoic before the wincing eyes, the rain
Of futile tears from multitudes in pain—
Knowing that this day's troubled flesh will pass
To spent dust under the impersonal grass—
Build in me, hills, the granite of your heart
That I may bear what rives my flesh apart;
Breed me as imperturbable and mute
To wretchedness as any stony butte;
Let fall your cowl of calm blue dusk on me,
The mantle of your cool tranquillity.

FOUR LITTLE FOXES

Speak gently, Spring, and make no sudden sound;
For in my windy valley, yesterday I found
New-born foxes squirming on the ground—
            Speak gently.

Walk softly, March, forbear the bitter blow;
Her feet within a trap, her blood upon the snow,
The four little foxes saw their mother go—
            Walk softly.

Go lightly, Spring, oh, give them no alarm;
When I covered them with boughs to shelter them from
    harm,
The thin blue foxes suckled at my arm—
            Go lightly.

Step softly, March, with your rampant hurricane;
Nuzzling one another, and whimpering with pain,
The new little foxes are shivering in the rain—
            Step softly.

FEATHER

High in the noon's bright bowl of blue
I saw an idling eagle tilt
His suave white wings; as smooth he flew
  As water flows on silt.

He wheeled; a feather from his wing
Fluttered from out the cloudless dome
And sank on the grassy carpeting,
  Soft as a moth on foam.

In the gravest hour before the dawn,
I heard, out of the star-flung height,
The gentle ghost of one long gone
  Whisper across the night.

The tender fragment of a call
Fell soft as the down of any bird.
And none, but I, saw the feather fall;
  And no man caught the word.

BROKEN DRAKE

Through harrowing hours now, O broken drake,
I've watched you from my shelter in these reeds,
Struggling to lift your splendor from this lake
That grips you, crippled, in a net of weeds.

How desperately you circle round and round
Your patch of open water in the rice,
Striving to break from chill white nights that hound
You down with inexorable inching ice.

What rending hunger in your calls, what fright,
When, wedge on wedge, the homing ducks swing low,
Gabbling their counsel to aid you in your plight,
To win you from the clutch of the grinding floe.

What flutter of shattered bone, what anguished cry
And frenzied frustrate lunge, O lonely thing,
When, wedge on wedge, they wheel and let you lie—
To sink back, panting, on your splintered wing.

Futile your hope; November night will crowd
You down to sleep on a green and glassy bed,
Cover you gently with a snowy shroud,
And chant for you in the rushes at your head.

HANG ME AMONG YOUR WINDS

Hang me among your winds, O God,
Above the tremulous stars,
Like a harp of quivering silver strings,
Showering, as it swings,
Its tuneful bars
Of eerie music on the earth.

Play over me, God,
Your cosmic melodies:
The gusty overture for Spring's
Caprice and wayward April's mirth;
The sensuous serenade
Of summer, languid in the alder glade;
The wistful symphonies
Of Autumn; and Winter's rhapsodies
Among the drifted dunes—
Her lullabies and her torrential tunes
Moody with wild cadenzas, with fitful stress
And poignant soundlessness.

Touch me, O God, with but a gesture—
And let each finger sweep
Over my strings until they leap
With life, and rain
Their silver chimes upon the plain,
In harmonies of far celestial spaces,
Of high and holy places.

8

FEUD

Poor wayworn creature! O sorely harried deer,
What drove you, quivering like a poplar-blade,
To refuge with my herd? What holds you here
Within my meadow, broken and afraid?

Tilting your nose to tainted air, you thrill
And freeze to wailing wolves! Fear you the sound
Of the coyotes eager for a tender kill?
Or yet the baying of the hunter's hound?

Let fall your anguish, harried one, and rest;
Bed yourself down among your kin, my cattle;
Sleep unperturbed, no spoiler shall molest
You here this night, for I shall wage your battle.

There was a day when coyotes in a pack,
Wolves of another hue, another breed,
With lust upon their lips, set out to track
Me down and drop me for my outcast creed.

O hunted creature, once I knew the thud
Of padded feet that put you into flight,
The bugle-cry, suffused with thundering blood,
That trembled in the brazen bell of night.

I knew your frenzied rocky run, the burst
Of lungs, the rivers of fire in every vein;
I knew your foaming lip, your boundless thirst,
The rain of molten-hammering in your brain.

9

Bide with me then, against the wolves' return,
For I shall carry on the feud for you;
And it shall be, to me, of small concern
If the wolf-hearts walk on four soft feet or two.

Oh, let them come! And I shall burn their flanks
With a blast of hell to end their revelry,
And whistle molten silver through their ranks,
Laughing—one round for you and one for me.

DEEP WET MOSS

Deep wet moss and cool blue shadows
    Beneath a bending fir,
And the purple solitude of mountains,
    When only the dark owls stir—
Oh, there will come a day, a twilight,
    When I shall sink to rest
In deep wet moss and cool blue shadows
    Upon a mountain's breast,
And yield a body torn with passions,
    And bruised with earthly scars,
To the cool oblivion of evening,
    Of solitude and stars.

ANGUS McGREGOR

Angus McGregor lies brittle as ice,
  With snow tucked up to his jaws,
Somewhere tonight where the hemlocks moan
  And crack in the wind like straws.

Angus went cruising the woods last month,
  With a blanket-roll on his back,
With never an ax, a dirk, a gun,
  Or a compass in his pack.

"The hills at thirty below have teeth;
  McGregor," I said, "you're daft
To tackle the woods like a simple child."
  But he looked at me and laughed.

He flashed his teeth in a grin and said:
  "The earth is an open book;
I've followed the woods for forty years,
  I know each cranny and crook.

"I've battled her weather, her winds, her brutes,
  I've stood with them toe to toe;
I can beat them back with my naked fist
  And answer them blow for blow."

Angus McGregor sleeps under the stars,
  With an icicle gripped in his hand,
Somewhere tonight where the grim-lipped peaks
  Brood on a haggard land.

Oh, the face of the moon is dark tonight,
  And dark the gaunt wind's sigh;
And the hollow laughter troubles me
  In the wild wolves' cry.

LET ME GO DOWN TO DUST

Let me go down to dust and dreams
Gently, O Lord, with never a fear
Of death beyond the day that is done;
In such a manner as beseems
A kinsman of the wild, a son
Of stoic earth whose race is run.
Let me go down as any deer,
Who, broken by a desperate flight,
Sinks down to slumber for the night—
Dumbly serene in certitude
That it will rise again at dawn,
Buoyant, refreshed of limb, renewed,
And confident that it will thrill
Tomorrow to its nuzzling fawn,
To the bugle-notes of elk upon the hill.

Let me go down to dreams and dust
Gently, O Lord, with quiet trust
And the fortitude that marks a child
Of earth, a kinsman of the wild.
Let me go down as any doe
That nods upon its ferny bed,
And, lulled to slumber by the flow
Of talking water, the muffled brawl
Of far cascading waterfall,
At last lets down its weary head
Deep in the brookmints in the glen;
And under the starry-candled sky,
With never the shadow of a sigh,
Gives its worn body back to earth again.

FRAIL BEAUTY

O molten dewdrop, trembling in the light
   Of dawn, and clinging to the brookmint-blade—
   A pendent opal on a breast of jade—
How came your splendor, so limpid and so bright?
How your clear symmetry? And what weird sleight
   Of art suffused you with each rainbow-shade,
   Captured your evanescent hour, and made
A quivering soul from fire and mist and night?

Fleeting your span! Yet I shall be content
   To let the Cosmic Power that built in you
Such frail wet beauty, such luster opulent,
   And such immortal life as lies in dew,
Fashion the fragile moment of my soul
In what frail shape It deems a perfect whole.

THE WORLD HAS A WAY WITH EYES

To Helen S.

Untroubled your eyes, O child, as ingenuous
And virginal as dew, as clear and clean,
Tranquil as mountain pools that hold the blue
  Of sky with never a blur between.

But there may come a day when ominous clouds
Will sully them; when the world's craft will touch
Their deeps and put in them the glint that lurks
  In the eyes of those who know too much.

The world has a way with eyes. Oh, eyes there are:
Eyes that forlornly fawn like mongrel dogs;
Or move as suavely as silt in a beaver-dam
  Flows over treacherous sunken logs;

Eyes that are cobwebbed windows in a house,
Deserted, bleak, where a soul once lived, and fled,
Behind whose drawn green shutters slippered ghosts
  Conjure among the diffident dead;

Men's eyes more cold than the stones in Pilate's skull;
Or as wistfully patient as the Crucified;
Eyes that are sullen ponds in whose dark depth
  Sinister green-lipped fishes glide.

Oh, the world has a way with eyes. Cling to me, child,
Here where the mountains surge to immaculate blue,

Where the winds blow pure and cool and the eagle soars;
  Let the wild sweet earth have its way with you.

Keep a long, long look on pine and peak that rise
Serene today, tomorrow—when the world's eyes go
To socketed dust; keep a long look on the hills.
  They know something, child, they know.

TO A GROVE OF SILVER BIRCHES

Good morning, lovely ladies! I've never seen
    You half so fair—I swear;
How beautiful your gowns of apple-green!
    And the ribbons in your hair!

What rapture do you await? What coming swain?
    Such rustling of petticoats!
Such wagging of heads and prinking in the rain!
    Such fluttering at your throats!

Dear winsome vestals, your flurry is no whim.
    I know your sly design;
And why the sap goes pulsing up each limb
    Sparkling as apple wine.

O ladies, trick you in your gala-best;
    For out of the ardent South,
Young April comes with a passion in his breast,
    And a kiss upon his mouth.

TO AN UGLY WHELP IN A LITTER OF WOLVES

Stony your portion, ugly whelp,
Here in this ravenous squealing brood
That scrambles for your mother's teats
    To drive at her dribbling food.

Poignant your whimper when you strive
To nose your dam, as your brother's jaws
Bead you with blood and drag you down
    To the litter's trampling paws.

Poor misfit, afterthought of God,
Creep to your corner from the slime,
Sleep with your one wistful eye
    Open, and bide your time.

Oh, there shall come a day—sweet day!—
When you will bolt the scourging pack
To stalk the bristling hills alone,
    Alone in the night's black.

The square-jawed crags will nurture you;
Adversity will forge your bone;
And winter keen your cunning—a knife
    Whetted upon a stone.

And there shall come a day—bright day!—
When wolves, banding in fright, will shun
The fangs of you and, at your snarl,
    Spew up their kills and run.

19

My neighbors, fearing an outlaw wolf,
A ruthless lobo, will polish the blue
Of their barrels on sounding moonlit nights
   And go gunning for you.

And you will tongue your battle-cry—
Grim challenge of the once buffoon!—
To every beast that walks or crawls
   Or flaps against the moon;

Your twisted silver laughter, deep
And darkly sprung from the throat of hell.
O starveling, we know the abysmal jest,
   We know the jest, and well.

OCTOBER GYPSY

Shake out your golden petticoats, October,
  And swirl your gown of dappled crimson leaves,
For soon you will see an end to joyous dancing—
    When the crafty hand of winter weaves
      A shroud about your sheaves.

O gypsy queen, arrayed in patterned fabrics
  Of pin-oaks blazing, of reeds and sedges brown,
Flutter your veils and jingle your bright medallions,
    Where glimmering sunlight filters down
      And spangles on your gown.

To the clatter of castanets among the rushes,
  Flash your curved limbs, O gypsy, toss your hips,
And stream upon the wind your ragged ribbons—
    Drunk with the sparkling wine that drips
      From the grape between your lips.

THE LOON

A lonely lake, a lonely shore,
A lone pine leaning on the moon;
All night the water-beating wings
Of a solitary loon.

With mournful wail from dusk to dawn
He gibbered at the taunting stars—
A hermit-soul gone raving mad,
And beating at his bars.

FLAME AND SMOKE

Of trivial concern my transient clay,
Flaming with fevers, falling in a day
To the baleful broken coal of pain and sorrow—
The flesh of yesterday, today, tomorrow.
The coddled bone and sinew, these shall pass
Down to cold embers, as any blazing mass.
Small consequence the body of the pyre,
The roaring boughs, the crackling ash, the fire.

Not so the flame that flesh may house, serene,
Nurtured by embers; the spirit tremulous, clean,
And sinewy-blue like the shadow of a soul
Eerily dancing on the dying coal.

As any blazing birchwood falls apart,
Groaning, consumed, and flings up from its heart
An essence that goes winding in a cloud,
In a ghostly flame within a smoking shroud—
So may I go, when my burning boughs crash
And nothing remains but feebly glowing ash,
And wisp of spirit spiraling and bending
Starward in tenuous flame and smoke ascending.

TETON MOUNTAIN

She walks alone against the dusky sky,
  With something of the manner of a queen—
Her gesturing peaks, imperious and high,
  Her snowy brown, serene.

Under her feet, a tapestry of pine;
  Veiling her marble figure, purple haze,
Draped with a scarf of clouds at timber-line,
  In a billowy silken maze.

And in the moonlight a spangled necklace shakes
  And shimmers silver-blue upon her shoulders—
A fragile thread of crinkling brooks and lakes
  In the glimmering ice and boulders.

Among her eagle-winged and starry host
  Of lovers, like an austere virgin nun,
She broods—yielding a moment at the most,
  To the lips of the ardent sun.

WAILING LYNX

What cry—from out the moonlit blue of wood—
   That lays the jagged crimson of a scar
Upon the face of this gaunt solitude
   And stabs each pallid star!

What ghostly terror this, that starts and spills
   Its tones from out the mountain's naked heart—
Whose echoes ricochet among the hills
   And cleave the sky apart!

BLACKTAIL DEER

The blacktail held his tawny marble pose,
With every supple muscle set to spring,
Nosing the tainted air—his slender limbs
And sinews like corded copper quivering.

Ponderous the minutes, while his smoldering eyes
Went burning over me, and searching mine;
His heart ticked off each moment as he stood
Waiting an ominous word, a sound, a sign.

I tossed a friendly gesture! The sinews snapped
And flung his bulk of rippled tawny stone
Over an alder, as when a bended pine,
Released from pressure, catapults a cone.

Bending an arch above the alder-crown,
In a stream of whistling wind the great buck went,
Flirting his tail in exclamation-marks
To punctuate his vast astonishment.

APRIL RAIN

Through a temperamental April night
I tossed upon my attic bed,
And gave myself to the rattle of rains
  On the gable overhead.

Rains of all moods slipped by: gray rains
That walked the eaves on panther paws;
Stony blue rains that scraped the tin
  With the sound of a grizzly's claws.

Whimpering rains that tried the latch
And fumbled at each window-hook,
Or slid with the belly of a snake
  Into each cranny and nook.

High-stepping rains like prancing steeds;
Rains that went galloping down the roof,
That shook the earth like buffalo-herds
  With thunder of flinty hoof.

The torrent ceased; and something dark
Depressed me, something in the dregs
Of April dripping from the eaves
  Into the rain-water kegs.

So hollow the sullen drop on drop,
So melancholy in the gloom,
I lit a candle and strove to drive
  The shadows from the room.

LET ME FLOWER AS I WILL

God, let me flower as I will!
For I am weary of the chill
Companionship of cloistered vines
And hothouse-nurtured columbines;
Oh, weary of the pruning-knife
That shapes my prim decorous life—
Of clambering trellises that hold me,
Of flawless patterned forms that mold me.

God, let me flower as I will!
A shaggy rambler on the hill—
Familiar with April's growing pain
Of green buds bursting after rain.
Oh, let me hear among the sheaves
Of autumn, the song of wistful leaves,
The lullaby of the brook that dallies
Among the high blue mountain valleys.
And may my comrades be but these:
Birds on the bough, and guzzling bees
Among my blossoms, as they sup
On the dew in my silver-petaled cup.

God, let my parching roots go deep
Among the cold green springs, and keep
Firm grip upon the mossy edges
Of imperishable granite ledges,
That thus my body may withstand
The avalanche of snow and sand,
The trample of the years, the flail
Of whipping wind and bouncing hail.

And when December with its shroud
Of fallen snow and leaden cloud,
Shall find me in the holiday
Of slumber, shivering and gray
Against the sky—and in the end,
My somber days shall hold no friend
But a whimpering wolf, and on the tree
A frozen bird—so may it be.
For in that day I shall have won
The glory of the summer sun;
My leaves, by windy fingers played,
An eerie music shall have made;
I shall have known in some far land
The tender comfort of a Hand,
And the liquid beauty of a Tongue
That finds its syllables among
Wild wind and waterfall and rill—
God, let me flower as I will!

THE WOLF CRY

The Arctic moon hangs overhead;
  The wide white silence lies below.
A starveling pine stands lone and gaunt,
  Black-penciled on the snow.

Weird as the moan of sobbing winds,
  A lone long call floats up from the trail;
And the naked soul of the frozen North
  Trembles in that wail.

THE GRANITE MOUNTAIN

To Carl Sandburg

I know a mountain, lone it lies
Under wide blue Arctic skies.

Gray against the crimson rags
Of sunset loom its granite crags.

Gray granite are the peaks that sunder
The clouds, and gray the shadows under.

Down the weathered gullies flow
Waters from its crannied snow:

Tumbling cataracts that roar
Cannonading down the shore;

And rivulets that hurry after
With a sound of silver laughter.

Up its ramparts winds a trail
To a clover-meadowed vale,

High among the hills and woods
Locked in lonely solitudes.

Only wild feet can essay
The perils of that cragged way.

And here beneath the rugged shoulders
Of the granite cliffs and boulders,

In the valley of the sky
Where tranquil twilight shadows lie,

Hunted creatures in their flight
Find a refuge for the night.

COYOTE BROOD

What a bewildering world is yours, wild brood,
Cringing before the north wind's surly mood,
And squirming as your mother's pink wet tongue
Licks the bedraggled fur of her new-born young.

Such eyes!—that come from darkness into day
Blinking and blinded by every sun-split ray,
Perplexed before the catastrophes of earth
That stalk you from the moment of your birth;

So overwhelmed by night, so round with wonder
When storm-clouds roll their drums in crashing thunder,
To summon you, like a strident challenge hurled,
To your battle for survival in this world.

Your span shall hold no respite from the pain
Of racking hunger, of stinging sleet and rain,
No loveliness but a moment of delight
Snatched in the sun or furtive in the night.

Goaded by fear that prods you like a knife,
Oh, not for you the complacencies of life;
Harried by belching steel and pitiless traps,
Your fondest hope is but a grim perhaps.

Into the world bewildered you were thrust,
To struggle bewildered with hate, disaster, lust;
Out of the world, defeated, driven, low,
To benevolent earth bewildered you will go.

ARTICULATE THRUSH

Oh, you and I, wild thrush—we share
The glory of this mountain slope:
Its hallowed dusk, its fragrant air,
    Its haze of heliotrope.

We know the high serenity
Of coming night: of the cool blue star,
Of the dewy tinkling bells from the lee
    Of the hills where the cattle are.

Not mine, but yours, the power to make
Articulate the prayer that wells
In every heart this hour, the ache
    Of beauty in these dells.

Chant then, O bird! Tilt back your bill;
Perched on the balsam's nodding cones,
From out the plum-blue shadows spill
    Your pebbly silver tones.

Speak to whatever Cosmic Power
Conjured to surging ecstasy
This day, its fire and dew and flower;
    And speak, sweet bird, for me.

MOUNTAIN HAMLET

Wide-eyed all night in the weather-worn inn,
As the bleak winds rattled on the rain-trough's tin,
Deep in a feather-bed I tossed in the gloom
That dripped from the walls of the attic room.

There was never a sound in the moldering house
But the wail of the wind and the squeak of a mouse
Eerily scampering under the gable . . .
Over the rafter . . . down on the table.

Never a sound but the slow tick-tock
From the laggard tongue of the grandfather's clock,
The bronchial whirr and the dubious chime
Of the old bronze bells as they croaked the time.

Remote I was from the face of a friend,
In a hamlet tucked where the mountains bend
A gnarly arm round a lonely sweep
So desolate that I could not sleep.

Restless, I crept to the window-sill:
The ice-browed cabins under the hill,
Forlorn, abandoned, huddled in a row
Like frozen ptarmigan squat in the snow.

The tavern lamplight, leaning on the blizzard,
Hooded in white, was a hunched-up wizard
With lean yellow fingers that conjured hosts
Of shambling shadows and slim gray ghosts.

35

I groped my way to the old bed-stead
And stared at the portrait over my head:
The long gone father of my host who was sleeping,
Snoring at ease, while the hours were creeping.

Through Gunflint Pass, with his old ox-cart,
He had reached this glade; with a resolute heart
He had swung his ax through these forest halls,
Had hewn the logs of these homestead walls.

Here in the hills, for seventy years,
This gaunt bell-wether of the pioneers
Had browsed content, and with placid eye
Had mulled his cud as the world rushed by.

And here, with his paunch and his apple-like face,
My host, his son—the last of his race—
Had slept untroubled by the slow tick-tock
And the dull bronze bells of his father's clock;

Had lived content, like his pioneer sire,
With his hickory-chair and his wide hearth-fire,
His cobwebbed kegs in the cellar's damp,
His feather-beds and his tavern-lamp.

I burrowed in my bed when a wintry gust
Clattered on the panes with a brittle white dust,
As the keen wind fumbled the flapping shutter
And moaned like a cat in the loose rain-gutter.

Soundless the mountain, soundless the wood,
Except for a lynx in the neighborhood,
Who shivered the night with a frozen wail
When the wind's teeth raked him from muzzle to tail.

Faintly I caught the struggle and strain,
The melancholy cry of a railway train
Climbing the Gunflint, high and higher,
The belly-born tones of the West Coast Flier.

Nearer the grinding clang and rattle
Of the transcontinental streaming to Seattle,
Whistling as she flew: "Make way! Make way!
For another tribe and another day!"—

Laden with vendors of motor-cars,
Radio experts and cinema stars,
With railway presidents, governors,
Airplane mechanics and realtors.

Like a red-tailed rocket in the midnight's black,
It crashed through the hamlet; and left in its track
The blinking eye of a signal-light
As its cloud of glory vanished in night.

The faint gold tones of its mellow bell—
Like the mumble of the sea held in a shell—
Trembled in the hills, so cupped and hollowed
They echoed the echoes. Silence followed.

Oh, never a sound but the groan of the floor—
Two ghostly feet at the inn-keeper's door . . .
Pacing the room of my host who sighed
And rolled on the bed where his father had died.

Never a sound but a squeak on the rafter,
The windmill's creak and the wind's wild laughter,
The interminable tick, the inevitable tock
Of the thick halt tongue of the grandfather's clock.

CLIPPED WINGS

Why do you flutter in my arms and scream,
O frenzied bird, as my poised blue scissors gleam
Above your outstretched wings, and wait to clip
From your shining mallard plumes each buoyant tip?

As I prepare to groom you for the stool
Of shorn decoys who swim my barnyard pool,
Do you by some vague intuition sense
The subtle coming of your impotence?

Never again will you rapturously tilt
Your wings to the sun to wash them in its gilt,
To wheel, and dizzily eddy down the expanse
Of blue to earth like a whistling fiery lance.

And ended the nights when the bayou lies asleep
And stars like silver minnows swim its deep—
Of breathless waiting, as your wild mate swings
Over your head and spreads her satin wings.

O wilding, the rebellion in your blood and bone
Doubles the constant anguish of my own—
Your fear of dark earth-fettered days to be,
Of a world whose sky-lines are a mockery;

A world of shallow barricaded ponds
That holds for you no shining blue beyonds,
No flaming high horizons to fire your breast
And send you bugling on a lofty quest.

Find comfort in this: if your proud wings are shorn
By my faltering blades, you shall wax fat with corn,
Drowse in the sun, and never know the bite
Of adversity again in day or night.

Shielded from every stealthy fox and hawk,
Contented on your puddle, you shall squawk
And find among my pens of placid geese,
Even as I, a soft seductive peace.

But when wild mallards stretch their vibrant throats
Against the moon and fling their brazen notes
Earthward to challenge and stop the hearts of all
Who grovel on earth, in a deep strong trumpet-call;

And when the frosted silver bell of sky
Rings with the rush of wings and the joyous cry
Of mallards streaming home, home again—
What then, O wretched sky-born bird, what then!

PART II

THE BOX OF GOD

THE BOX OF GOD*

I

BROKEN BIRD

O broken bird,
Whose whistling silver wings have known the lift
Of high mysterious hands, and the wild sweet music
Of big winds among the ultimate stars!—
The black-robed curés put your pagan Indian
Soul in their white man's House of God, to lay
Upon your pagan lips new songs, to swell
The chorus of amens and hallelujahs.
In simple faith and holy zeal, they flung
Aside the altar-tapestries, that you
Might know the splendor of God's handiwork,
The shining glory of His face. O eagle,
Crippled of pinion, clipped of soaring wing,
They brought you to a four-square box of God;
And they left you there to flutter against the bars
In futile flying, to beat against the gates,
To droop, to dream a little, and to die.

Ah, Joe Shing-ób—by the sagamores revered
As Spruce, the Conjurer, by the black-priests dubbed
The Pagan Joe—how clearly I recall
Your conversion in the Big-Knife's House of God,
Your wonder when you faced its golden glories.
Don't you remember?—when first you sledged from out

* For supplementary comments on this poem, and on other Indian
themes, see *Appendix,* page 332.

43

The frozen Valley of the Sleepy-eye,
And hammered on the gates of Fort Brazeau—
To sing farewell to Áh-nah-qúod, the Cloud,
Sleeping, banked high with flowers, clothed in the pomp
Of white man's borrowed garments, in the church?
Oh, how your heart, as a child's heart beating before
High wonder-workings, thrilled at the burial splendor!—
The coffin, shimmering-black as moonlit ice,
And gleaming in a ring of waxen tapers;
After the chant of death, the long black robes,
Blown by the wind and winding over the hills
With slow black songs to the marked-out-place-of-death;
The solemn feet that moved along the road
Behind the wagon-with-windows, the wagon-of-death,
With its jingling silver harness, its dancing plumes.
Oh, the shining splendor of that burial march,
The round-eyed wonder of the village throng!—
And oh, the fierce-hot hunger, the burning envy
That seared your soul when you beheld your friend
Achieve such high distinction from the black-robes!

And later, when the cavalcade of priests
Wound down from the fenced-in ground, like a slow black
    worm
Crawling upon the snow—don't you recall?—
The meeting in the mission?—that night, your first
In the white man's lodge of holy-medicine?
How clearly I can see your hesitant step
On the threshold of the church; within the door
Your gasp of quick surprise, your breathless mouth;
Your eyes round-white before the glimmering taper,

44

The golden-filigreed censer, the altar hung
With red rosettes and velvet soft as an otter's
Pelt in the frost of autumn, with tinsel sparkling
Like cold blue stars above the frozen snows.
Oh, the blinding beauty of that House of God!—
Even the glittering bar at Jock McKay's,
Tinkling with goblets of fiery devil's-spit,
With dazzling vials and many-looking mirrors,
Seemed lead against the silver of the mission.

I hear again the chanting holy-men,
The agents of the white man's Mighty Spirit,
Making their talks with strong, smooth-moving tongues:

"Hear! Hear ye, men of a pagan faith!
Forsake the idols of your heathen fathers,
The too-many ghosts that walk upon the earth;
For there lie pain and sorrow, yea, and death!

"Hear! Hear ye, men of a pagan faith!
And grasp the friendly hands we offer you
In kindly fellowship, warm hands and tender,
Yea, hands that ever give and never take.
Forswear the demon-charms of medicine-men;
Shatter the drums of conjuring Chée-sah-kée—
Yea, beyond these walls lie bitterness and death!

"Pagans!—ye men of a bastard birth!—bend;
Bow ye, proud heads, before this hallowed shrine!
Break!—break ye the knee beneath this roof,
For within this house lives God! Abide ye here.

45

Here shall your eyes behold His wizardry;
Here shall ye find an everlasting peace."

Ah, Joe the pagan, son of a bastard people,
Child of a race of vanquished, outlawed children,
Small wonder that you drooped your weary head,
Blinding your eyes to the suns of elder days;
For hungry bellies look for new fat gods,
And heavy heads seek newer, softer pillows.
With you again I hear the eerie chants
Floating from out the primal yesterdays—
The low sweet song of the doctor's flute, the slow
Resonant boom of the basswood water-drum,
The far voice of the fathers, calling, calling.
I see again the struggle in your eyes—
The hunted soul of a wild young grouse, afraid,
Trembling beneath maternal wings, yet lured
By the shrill whistle of the wheeling hawk.
I see your shuffling limbs, hesitant, faltering
Along the aisle—the drag of old bronzed hands
Upon your moccasined feet, the forward tug
Of others, soft and white, and very tender;
One forward step . . . another . . . a quick look back!—
Another step . . . another . . . and lo! the eyes
Flutter and droop before a flaming symbol,
The strong knees break before a blazoned altar
Glimmering its tapestries in the candle-light,
The high head beaten down and bending before
New wonder-working images of gold.

And thus the black-robes brought you into the house
Wherein they kept their God, a house of logs,

Square-hewn, and thirty feet by forty. They strove
To put before you food and purple trappings—
Oh, how they walked you up and down in the vestry
Proudly resplendent in your white man's raiment,
Glittering and gorgeous, the envy of your tribe:
Your stiff silk hat, your scarlet sash, your shoes
Shining and squeaking gloriously with newness!
Yet even unto the end—those blood-stained nights
Of the Sickness-on-the-lung; that bitter day
On the Barking-rock, when I packed you down from camp
At Split-hand Falls to the fort at Sleepy-eye;
While, drop by drop, your life went trickling out,
As sugar-sap that drips on the birch-bark bucket
And finally chills in the withered maple heart
At frozen dusk: even unto the end—
When the mission doctor, framed by guttering candles,
Hollowly tapped his hooked-horn finger here
And there upon your bony breast, like a wood-bird
Pecking and drumming on a rotten trunk—
Even unto this end I never knew
Which part of you was offering the holy prayers—
The chanting mouth, or the eyes that gazed beyond
The walls to a far land of windy valleys.
And sometimes, when your dry slow lips were moving
To perfumed psalms, I could almost, almost see
Your pagan soul aleap in the fire-light, naked,
Shuffling along to booming medicine-drums,
Shaking the flat black earth with moccasined feet,
Dancing again—back among the jangling
Bells and the stamping legs of gnarled old men—

47

Back to the fathers calling, calling across
Dead winds from the dim gray years.

                     O high-flying eagle,
Whose soul, wheeling among the sinuous winds,
Has known the molten glory of the sun,
The utter calm of dusk, and in the evening
The lullabies of moonlit mountain waters!—
The black-priests locked you in their House of God,
Behind great gates swung tight against the frightened
Quivering aspens, whispering perturbed in council,
And muttering as they tapped with timid fists
Upon the doors and strove to follow you
And hold you; tight against the uneasy winds
Wailing among the balsams, fumbling upon
The latch with fretful fingers; tight against
The crowding stars who pressed their troubled faces
Against the windows. In honest faith and zeal,
The black-robes put you in a box of God,
To swell the broken chorus of amens
And hallelujahs; to flutter against the door
Crippled of pinion, bruised of head; to beat
With futile flying against the gilded bars;
To droop, to dream a little, and to die.

II

WHISTLING WINGS

Shing-ób, companion of my old wild years
In the land of K'tchée-gah-mee, my good right arm
When we battled bloody-fisted in the storms

48

And snows with rotting scurvy, with hunger raw
And ravenous as the lusting tongues of wolves—
My Joe, no longer will the ghostly mountains
Echo your red-lunged laughters in the night;
The gone lone days when we communed with God
In the language of the waterfall and wind
Have vanished with your basswood water-drum.

Do you recall our cruise to Flute-reed Falls?
Our first together—oh, many moons ago—
Before the curés built the village mission?
How, banked against our camp-fire in the bush
Of sugar-maples, we smoked kín-nik-kin-ník,
And startled the somber buttes with round raw songs,
With wails that mocked the lynx who cried all night
As if her splitting limbs were torn with the pain
Of a terrible new litter? How we talked
Till dawn of the Indian's Kéetch-ie Má-ni-dó,
The Mighty Spirit, and of the white man's God?—
Don't you remember dusk at Cold-spring Hollow?—
The beaver-pond at our feet, its ebony pool
Wrinkled with silver, placid, calm as death,
Save for the fitful chug of the frog that flopped
His yellow jowls upon the lily-pad,
And the quick wet slap of the tails of beaver hurrying
Homeward across the furrowing waters, laden
With cuttings of tender poplar . . . down in the swale
The hermit-thrush who spilled his rivulet
Of golden tones into the purple seas
Of gloam among the swamps . . . and in the East,
Serene against the sky—do you remember?—

Slumbering Mont du Père, shouldering its crags
Through crumpled clouds, rose-flushed with afterglow . . .
And dew-lidded dusk that slipped among the valleys
Soft as a blue wolf walking in thick wet moss.
How we changed our ribald song for simple talk! . . .

> "My frien', Ah-déek, you ask-um plenty hard question:
> Ugh! w'ere Kéetch-ie Má-ni-dó he live?
> W'ere all dose Eenzhun spirits walk and talk?
> Me—I dunno! . . . Mebbe . . . mebbe over here,
> In beaver-pond, in t'rush, in gromping bullfrog;
> Mebbe over dere, he's sleeping in dose mountain. . . .

> "Sh-sh-sh! . . . Look!—over dere—look, my frien'!
> On Mont du Père—he's moving little! . . . ain't?
> Under dose soft blue blanket she's falling down
> On hill and valley! Somebody—somebody's dere!
> In dose hill of Mont du Père, sleeping . . . sleeping . . ."

And when the fingers of the sun, lingering,
Slipped gently from the marble brow of the glacier
Pillowed among the clouds, blue-veined and cool,
How, one by one, like lamps that flicker up
In a snow-bound hamlet in the valley, the stars
Lighted their candles mirrored in the waters . . .
And floating from the hills of Sleepy-eye,
Soft as the wings of dusty-millers flying,
The fitful syllables of the Baptism River
Mumbling among its caverns hollowly,
Shouldering its emerald sweep through cragged cascades
In a flood of wafted foam, fragile, flimsy
As luna-moths fluttering on a pool . . .

50

"You hear dat, Caribou? . . . somebody's dere! . . .
Ain't?—in dose hills of Mont du Père—sleeping.
Sh-sh-sh! You hear dose far 'way Flute-reed Falls?
Somebody's dere in Mont du Père, sleeping . . .
Somebody he's in dere de whole night long . . .
And w'ile he's sleep, he's talking little . . . talking . . ."

Hush!—don't you hear K'tchée-gah-mee at midnight?—
That stretched far out from the banks of Otter-slide
To the dim wet rim of the world—South, East, West?—
The Big-water, calm, thick-flecked with the light of stars
As the wind-riffled fur of silver fox in winter . . .
The shuffle of the sands in the lapsing tide . . .
The slow soft wash of waters on the pebbles . . .

"Sh-sh-sh! . . . Look Ah-déek!—on K'tchée-gah-mee!
Somebody—somet'ing he's in dere . . . ain't? . . .
He's sleep w'ere black Big-water she's deep . . . Ho!
In morning he's jump up from hees bed and race
Wit' de wind; tonight he's sleeping . . . rolling little—
Dreaming about hees woman . . . rolling . . . sleeping . . ."

And later—you recall?—beyond the peaks
That tusked the sky like fangs of a coyote snarling,
The full-blown mellow moon that floated up
Like a liquid-silver bubble from the waters,
Serenely, till she pricked her delicate film
On the slender splinter of a cloud, melted,
And trickled from the silver-dripping edges.
Oh, the splendor of that night! . . . the Twin-fox stars
That loped across the pine-ridge . . . Red Ah-núng,

Blazing from out the cavern of the gloom
Like the smouldering coal in the eye of carcajou . . .
The star-dust in the valley of the sky,
Flittering like glow-worms in a reedy meadow! . . .

"Somebody's dere . . . He's walk-um in dose cloud . . .
You see-um? Look! He's mak'-um for hees woman
De w'ile she sleep, dose t'ing she want-um most—
Blue dress for dancing! You see, my frien'? . . . ain't?
He's t'rowing on de blanket of dose sky
Dose plenty-plenty handfuls of w'ite stars;
He's sewing on dose plenty teet' of elk,
Dose shiny looking-glass and plenty beads.
Somebody's dere . . . somet'ing he's in dere . . ."

Thus the green moons went—and many, many winters.
Yet we held together, Joe, until our day
Of falling leaves, like two split sticks of bur-oak
Lashed tight with buckskin buried in the bark.
Do you recollect our last long cruise together,
To Hollow-bear, on our line of beaver-traps?—
When cold Bee-bóan, the Winter-maker, hurdling
The rim-rock ridge, shook out his snowy hair
Before him on the wind and heaped up the hollows?—
Flanked by the drifts, our lean-to of toboggans,
Our bed of pungent balsam, soft as down
From the bosom of a wild gray goose in autumn . . .
Our steaming sledge-dogs buried in the snow-bank,
Nuzzling their snouts beneath their tented tails,
And dreaming of the paradise of dogs . . .
Our fire of pine-boughs licking up the snow,

And tilting at the shadows in the coulee . . .
And you, rolled warm among the beaver-pelts,
Forgetful of your Sickness-on-the-lung,
Of the fever-pains and coughs that racked your bones—
You, beating a war song on your drum,
And laughing as the scarlet-moccasined flames
Danced on the coals and billowed up the sky.

Don't you remember? . . . the snowflakes drifting down
Thick as the falling petals of wild plums . . .
The clinker-ice and the scudding fluff of the whirlpool
Muffling the summer-mumblings of the brook . . .
The turbulent waterfall protesting against
Such early winter-sleep, like a little boy
Who struggles with the calamity of slumber,
Knuckling his leaden lids and his tingling nose
With a pudgy fist, and fretfully flinging back
His snowy covers with his petulant fingers.
Out on the windy barrens restless bands
Of caribou, rumped up against the gale,
Suddenly breaking before the rabid blast,
Scampering off like tumbleweeds in a cyclone . . .
The low of bulls from the hills where worried moose,
Nibbling the willows, the wintergreens, the birches,
Were yarding up in the sheltering alder-thicket . . .
From the cedar wind-break, the bleat of fawns wedged warm
Against the bellies of their drowsy does . . .
And then the utter calm . . . the wide white drift
That lay upon the world as still and ghastly
As the winding-sheet of death . . . the sudden snap
Of a dry twig . . . the groan of sheeted rivers

53

Beating with naked hands upon the ice . . .
The brooding night . . . the crackle of cold skies . . .

"Sh-sh-sh! . . . Look, my frien'—somebody's dere!
Ain't? . . . over dere? He's come from Land-of-Winter!
Wit' quilt he's cover-um up dose baby mink,
Dose cub, dose wild arbutus, dose jump-up-Johnny . . .
He's keep hees chil'ens warm for long, long winter . . .
Sh-sh-sh! . . . Somebody's dere on de w'ite savanna!
Somebody's dere! . . . He's walk-um in de timber . . .
He's cover-um up hees chil'ens, soft . . . soft . . ."

And later, when your bird-claw fingers rippled
Over the holes of your cedar bée-bee-gwún
Mellowly in a tender tune, how the stars,
Like little children trooping from their teepees,
Danced with their nimble feet across the sky
To the running-water music of your flute . . .
And how, with twinkling heels they scurried off
Before the Northern Light swaying, twisting,
Spiralling like a slender silver smoke
On the thin blue winds, and feeling out among
The frightened starry children of the sky . . .

"Look!—in de Land-of-Winter—somet'ing's dere!
Somebody—he's reaching out hees hand!—for me!
Ain't? . . . For me he's waiting. Somebody's dere!
Somebody he's in dere, waiting . . . waiting . . ."

Don't you remember?—the ghostly silence, splintered
At last by a fist that cracked the hoary birch,

54

By a swift black fist that shattered the brittle air,
Splitting it into a million frosty fragments . . .
And dreary Northwind, coughing in the snow,
Spitting among the glistening sheeted pines,
And moaning on the barrens among the bones
Of gaunt white tamaracks mournful and forlorn . . .

> *"Sh-sh-sh-sh! . . . My Caribou! Somebody's dere!*
> *He's crying . . . little bit crazy in dose wind . . .*
> *Ain't? . . . You hear-um . . . far 'way . . . crying*
> *Lak my old woman w'en she's lose de baby*
> *And no can find-um—w'en she's running everyw'ere*
> *Falling in snow, talking little bit crazy,*
> *Calling and crying for shees little boy . . .*
> *Sh-sh-sh! . . . Somet'ing's dere—you hear-um? . . . ain't?*
> *Somebody—somebody's dere, crying . . . crying . . ."*

Then from the swale, where shadows pranced grotesquely
Solemn, like phantom puppets on a string,
A cry—pointed, brittle, perpendicular—
As startling as a thin stiff blade of ice
Laid swift and sharp on fever-burning flesh:
The tremulous wail of a lonely shivering wolf,
Piercing the world's great heart like an icy sword . . .

> *"Look! . . . Quick!—Ah-déek! . . . Somebody's dere!*
> *Ain't? . . . He's come—he's come for me—for me!*
> *Me—me, I go! . . . . My Caribou—*
> *Dose fire—dose fire she's going out—she's cold . . .*
> *T'row—t'row on dose knots of pine . . . Mee-gwétch!*
> *And pull 'way from dose flame—dose pan of sour-dough,*
> *If you want eat—in de morning—plenty good flapjack.*

"Sh-sh-sh-sh! Somet'ing's dere! . . . You hear-um? ain't?
Somebody—somebody's dere, calling . . . calling . . .
I go . . . . . I go—me! . . . . . me . . . . . I go. . . ."

III

TALKING WATERS

O eagle whose whistling wings have known the lift
Of high mysterious hands, and the wild sweet music
Of big winds among the ultimate stars,
The black-robes put you in a box of God,
Seeking in honest faith and holy zeal
To lay upon your lips new songs, to swell
The chorus of amens and hallelujahs.
O bundle of copper bones tossed in a hole,
Here in the place-of-death—God's-fenced-in-ground!—
Beneath these put-in-pines and waxen lilies,
They placed you in a crimson gash in the hillside,
Here on a bluff above the Sleepy-eye,
Where the Baptism River, mumbling among the canyons,
Shoulders its flood through crooning waterfalls
In a mist of wafted foam fragile as petals
Of windflowers blowing across the green of April;
Where ghosts of wistful leaves go floating up
In the rustling blaze of autumn, like silver smokes
Slenderly twisting among the thin blue winds;
Here in the great gray arms of Mont du Père,
Where the shy arbutus, the mink, and the Johnny-jump-up
Huddle and whisper of a long, long winter;
Where stars, with soundless feet, come trooping up
To dance to the water-drums of white cascades—

Where stars, like little children, go singing down
The sky to the flute of the wind in the willow-tree—
Somebody—somebody's there . . . O Pagan Joe . . .
Can't you see Him? as He moves among the mountains?
Where dusk, dew-lidded, slips among the valleys
Soft as a blue wolf walking in thick wet moss?
Look!—my friend!—at the breast of Mont du Père! . . .
Sh-sh-sh-sh! . . . Don't you hear His talking waters? . . .
Soft in the gloom as broken butterflies
Hovering above a somber pool . . . Sh-sh-sh-sh!
Somebody's there . . . in the heart of Mont du Père . . .
Somebody—somebody's there, sleeping . . . sleeping . . .

PART III

TRAILING ARBUTUS

For M. H. S.

TUMULTUOUS MOMENT

Your eyes, O love, that melt and swim—
Like any tremulous mating doe's
In autumn—blazing, abrim,
Molten with ardors that disclose
The terrible compulsion of your flesh; your eyes—
Cleaving to mine with love as fell
As deep green waters in a well;
Your eyes, suffusing impetuously
With tides that fall and rise
Ungoverned as the bare abandoned sea
Yielding upon a fluid sand,
Ungovernable as the surge
And lapse of the sea beneath the moon's urge;
Your eyes, your every ravishing feature—
Who can deny them! or long withstand
The anguished beat and break of them! O lovely creature!

FAMILIAR WINGS

Oh, I shall wait for you,
Among these tilting pines
That lock their marching lines
And lean their lances on the moon;
Wait for you here, like any loon
That mourns upon the white
Of moonlit water and shakes the night
With the trembling echoes of his sorrow;
Oh, I shall wait for you—
Tomorrow and tomorrow—
As any loon that rings
His anguish skyward tone by tone
May wait forlorn, alone,
For the coming music of sweet familiar wings.

PEELED POPLAR

Slumbering upon her snowy bed
With a candle at her head,
So immaculately nude,
Supple of thigh and trim,
So delicate, so slim—
My love is beautiful;
Silkenly soft of limb
And rounded shoulder, ivory-hued
Against the smoky-velvet night
That stretches out beyond
The rosy ring of candle-light,
She is lovely—oh, beautiful
As any peeled wet poplar wand,
As satin-smooth and cool.

And there are hours of blight,
When gnawing griefs infest
My heart and sorrow is my guest—
When fevers that consume me pour
Stormily through my mesh
Of bursting vein and flesh
Like rivers of molten ore—
Oh, there are hours
When I can scarcely speak—
So sharp is my delight
In touching cool wet white,
When peeled wet wood is pressed
Against my burning cheek
Or touches my hot breast.

LONELY AS A BIRD

Lonely, oh, lonely as a hermit-thrush
   Freighting the gloomy spruce with grief,
I long for you and yearn in the twilight hush
   For the rustle of a leaf.

Lonely, oh, lonely, as a wistful bird
   Mocked by the night and the wind's laughter,
I call, and await your gentle cry, your word . . .
   To know only echoes after.

SO LIKE A QUIET RAIN

So like a rain she seems, a soothing rain
Tapping cool fingers on a window-pane,
And dropping syllables more slow and soft
Than the talk of sleepy pigeons in a loft.

NIGHT LETTER

Written in a Hospital

Please don't come, my dear,
To this forlorn vast solitude;
Oh, let me be—alone—
To rest, to stifle pain,
To sleep untroubled
Until I find my wings again.

Oh, my dear,
Don't doubt that I love you.
I do! I do! . . .

But—
How can I explain
My surface perversity!

Perhaps—

Do you recollect the October dawn
When we went paddling down the Rolling-stone,
Hunting wild ducks together?
The morning of the first big flight
Of mallards, blue-bills, widgeons?
(How beautiful you were!
Your slender throat,
Your chiseled-marble chin,
Your delicately ardent lips.)

Do you recall the mallard flock
That wheeled and whistled above our heads

So suddenly that it took our breath away?
And how, astonished, awkwardly I leaped
To clutch my gun and let them have a volley?—
If the fickle canoe had tossed another inch
Under my clumsy boots,
I'd have been forced to dive
Or tip up like a feeding duck,
To salvage our sodden luncheon
Before the fish waxed fat on it.

The single mallard drake, the green-head—
Remember?—who crumpled up his wings,
Plummeted down from out the clouds,
And crashed upon the surface of the lake,
Mangled, bleeding, broken,
But alive—alive.

How desperately he swam to shore, poor devil,
Dragging his shattered wings,
And clambered up the rushy bank
For refuge in the maze of sheltering reeds—
And for something, something more.

Oh, I knew why—for what! I knew!
It was the mallard's way—
And in the blood of every bruised wild thing,
Of every broken son of earth—
The mallard's way: to drag
His broken splendor to a niche,
To lie among the rushes quietly,
Alone . . . alone . . .

Patiently, dumbly, untroubled, undisturbed,
With never a cry, a call, a moan in his throat;
Waiting . . . waiting . . .
Until the earth renews his blood again,
His futile wings, and bids him soar;
Waiting . . . waiting . . .
Until the breath runs gently out of him,
And nodding low and lower inch by inch,
He sinks at last to dark and ultimate sleep.

Please!—no tears for me,
No gesture of grief,
No sigh, no fluttering of despair;
Oh, no more weeping,
No more melancholy prayer,
Than if I were a lone drake . . . waiting.

PART IV

TAMARACK BLUE

TAMARACK BLUE

As any brush-wolf, driven from the hills
By winter famine, waits upon the fringe
Of a settlement for cover of the dusk,
And enters it by a furtive, devious route,
Cowering among the shadows, freezing taut
With every sound—so came the widow Blue
In winter-moons to parish Pointe aux Trembles,
Doubled to earth beneath her pack of furs,
To ply her trade, to barter at the Post.
And if she ventured near the village inn,
Baring their yellow tusks the roustabouts
Would toss a dry slow leer at her and stone
Old Tamarack numb with "Mag, the Indian hag,"
With ribald epithet and jibe and gesture.
And when they waxed melodious with rum,
Pounding their ribs, and knew no way to free
The head of steam that hammered in their breasts,
Save in a raucous music, they would blare:
"She wears for a petticoat a gunny bag"—
Adding, with many ponderous knowing winks,
"Oh, Skinflint Blue, with a shin of flint, too";
And thus to the end they thumped their maudlin song
With laughter raw, big-bellied. There were days
When the Christian gentlemen of Pointe aux Trembles
Would welcome Tamarack with such fusillade
Of bilious humor that the harried squaw,
Bruised by their epithets, with swimming eyes
Intent upon the dust, seemed well-nigh gone,
Stoned to the earth; there came a stumbling hour

When I put an arm around her bag of ribs,
And felt her bosom pounding with such fear
That had I dared to place my weight of thumb
Upon her heart, I could have pressed the life
From her as from a fluttering crippled wren
Held in my hand.

          Nor was the widow's perfume
Of name and reputation without reason:
Penurious, forgetful of her own
Hungering flesh, she strangled every coin
And hoarded it against some secret need;
And slattern she was—a juiceless crone, more drab
To contemplate than venison long-cured
By the slow smoke of burning maple logs—
And quite as pungent with the wilderness.
What with the fight to draw the sap of life
From grudging toil, in sun and wind and snow,
Twenty-one years of Indian widowhood
Will parch a soul and weather any hide
To the texture of a withered russet apple:
A moon of hauling sap in the sugar-bush,
Of boiling maple-syrup; a moon for netting
Whitefish and smoking them upon the racks;
Two moons among the berries, plums, and cherries;
A moon in the cranberry bog; another moon
For harvesting the wild rice in the ponds;
Odd days for trailing moose and jerking meat;
And then the snow—and trap-lines to be strung
Among the hills for twenty swampy miles,
For minks and martens, otters, beavers, wolves.

So steadfast was the bronzed coureuse de bois
On her yearly round—like hands upon a clock—
Given the week and weather, I could tell
As surely as the needle of a compass
Finds the magnetic pole, what grove of spruce,
What jutting rock or lonely waste of swamp
Sheltered the widow's bones at night from beat
Of rain or snow.

              And when the spring thaws came,
And bread was low, and her pagan stomach lay
As flat against her spine as any trout's
After a spawning-season, there were nights
When Tamarack's ears were sensitive to silver—
Evenings when any lumberjack on drive,
Gone rampant with the solitude of winter
And hungry for affection, might persuade
The otherwise forlorn and famished widow
To join him in a moment of romance.
Oh, not without demurring did she yield—
And not without reason: otter pelts are rare,
Cranberries buy no silken petticoats,
No singing lessons—for there was Susie Blue.

Whenever Tamarack touched the world in shame
Or drudgery or barter, she had for end
The wringing of a comfort for her daughter—
As when a cactus pushes down its roots
Among the hostile sands for food and moisture,
And sends the stream and sparkle of its life
Up to a creaming blossom. None of us

73

In parish Pointe aux Trembles could fathom why
The outcast crucified herself for Susie.
Some said that Susie Blue was all the kin
The starveling had; and others, among the elders,
Held that the half-breed daughter carried every
Feature of Antoine Blue, who fathered her,
As clearly as a tranquil mountain-pool
Holds on its breast the overhanging sky;
And added that the pagan drab was proud
That she had crossed to the issue of her flesh
The pure white strain, the color of a Frenchman.
Whatever the reason, when the voyageur
Let out his quart of blood upon the floor
After a drunken brawl at Jock McKay's,
The widow set herself to live for Susie,
Bustling from crimson dawn to purple dusk—
And sometimes in the furtive black of night—
Hither and yon, in every wind and weather,
Scratching the mulch for morsels of the earth,
And salvaging the tender bits—a grouse
With a solitary chick. Of luxuries
Wrung from the widow's frame there was no end:
Ribbons and scarves and laces—all for Susie;
And four long years at Indian boarding-school;
A year at Fort de Bois in business-college
For higher education; and, topping all,
Three seasons spent in culture of the voice.
Oh, such a dream as stirred the widow's heart!—
A hope that put a savor in her world,
A zest for life; a dream of cities thralled
By silver music fountaining from Susie,

Cities that flashed upon the velvet night
In scrawling fire the name of Susie Blue;
A dream wherein the widow would declare
In glory, comfort, rest, her dividends
Upon the flesh put in for capital.

How clearly I recall the eventful spring
When Sue returned from her gilding at the Fort!
Old Tamarack was away—at Lac la Croix
Netting for fish—and could not come to town
To welcome her. But when the run of trout
Was at an end, she cached her nets and floats
And paddled down in time for Corpus Christi.
Some circumstance conspired to keep the two
Apart until the eucharistic feast—
Perhaps the village folk who always took
A Christian interest in Susie's morals.
But Thursday found the wistful derelict
Stiff on a bench in Mission Sacré Coeur
More taut for the high sweet moment of her life
Than quivering catgut strung upon a fiddle—
For Susie was to sing in Corpus Christi;
The pagan was about to claim her own.

I'd never seen the squaw in her Sunday-best:
Soft doeskin moccasins of corn-flower blue,
Patterned with lemon beads and lemon quills;
Checkered vermilion gown of calico
To hide her flinty shins, her thin flat hips;
An umber shawl, drawn tight about her head
And anchored at her breast by leather hands—

A dubious madonna of the pines.
Somehow the crone had burst her dull cocoon
Upon this day, was almost radiant
With loveliness, as if upon the new-born
Wings of desire she were about to leave
The earth and know the luxury of sunlight.
The apologetic eyes, the mien of one
Bludgeoned to earth by rancid drollery,
Had vanished; on her face there was the look
That glorifies a partridge once in life—
When, after endless labor, pain, and trouble
Rearing her first-born brood, she contemplates
Her young ones pattering among the leaves
On steady legs, and, clucking pridefully,
Outspreads her shining feathers to the wind.
And when the widow shot a wisp of smile
At me from underneath her umber cowl—
A smile so tremulous, so fragmentary,
And yet so shyly confident that all
The dawning world this day was exquisite,
A whisk of overture so diffident
And yet so palpitant for friendliness—
Somehow the poignant silver of it slipped
Between my ribs and touched me at the quick,
And I was moved to join her in her pew.

Oh, how her eyes, like embers in a breeze,
Flared up to life when Father Bruno led
Her daughter from the choir and Susie set
Herself to sing. Susie was beautiful,
Sullenly beautiful with sagging color:

Blue was the half-seen valley of her breast;
Her blue hair held the dusk; beneath her lids
Blue were the cryptic shadows, stealthy blue,
Skulking with wraiths that spoke of intimate,
Too intimate, communion with the night,
The languor of the moon. Beneath the glass
Of hothouse culture she had come to fruit,
A dusky grape grown redolent with wine,
A grape whose velvet-silver bloom reveals
The finger-smudge of too many dawdling thumbs.

She braced herself and tossed a cataract
Of treble notes among the mission rafters,
While Sister Mercy followed on the organ.
Something distressed me in the melody—
A hint of metal, a subtle dissonance;
Perhaps the trouble lay with Sister Mercy,
Or else the organ needful of repair.
To me there seemed a mellow spirit wanting,
As if the chambers of the half-breed's soul—
Like a fiddle-box, unseasoned by the long
Slow sun and wind, and weathered too rapidly
Beside a comfortable hothouse flame—
Lacked in the power to resonate the tone.
But the widow sat beatified, enthralled;
To her the cold flat notes were dulcet-clear,
As golden in their tones as the slow bronze bell
That swung among the girders overhead
And echoed in the hills. And Susie sang,
Serene, oblivious of all the world—
Save in a dim far pew a florid white man

77

Whose glance went up her bosom to her lips
And inventoried all of Susie's charms.
Was it for him she chanted? lifted up
The tawny blue-veined marble of her arm
In a casual gesture to pat a random lock?
For him she shook her perfume on the air?—
Bold as a young deer rutting in October,
Drenching its heavy musk upon the wind,
And waiting—silhouetted on the moon—
Waiting the beat of coming cloven hoofs.

When Sue dispatched her final vibrant note
In a lingering amen and came to earth,
She undulated down the aisle with a swash
Of silken petticoat to greet and join
Her glorified old mother—so it seemed.
And when she came within the pagan's reach,
The widow, bright with tears, and tremulous,
Uttered a rivulet of ecstasy
As wistful as the wind in autumn boughs,
And strove to touch the hand of Sue, half stood
To welcome her. The daughter paused, uncertain,
The passing of a breath. Haunted her face;
The dear dim ghosts of wildwood yesterdays
Laid gentle hands upon the half-breed's heart,
Struggled to bring her soul to life again.
She wavered. Then conscious of the battery
Of parish eyes on her, the village code
Rich with taboos of blue and flinty flesh,
And mindful of the gulf between the two,
Sprung from her Christian culture at the Fort,

78

She gathered up her new-born pride, and froze.
With eyes as cold and stony as a pike's
She looked at Tamarack—as on a vagrant wind;
With but the tremor of a lip, a fleeting
Hail and farewell, she slipped her flaccid palm
From out the pagan's gnarled and weathered hand
And rustled down the room and out the door,
The stranger at her heels—a coyote warm
And drooling on the trail of musky deer.

The widow held her posture, breathless, stunned;
Swayed for a moment, blindly groped her way,
And wilted to the bench—as when a mallard,
High on a lift of buoyant homing wind,
Before a blast of whistling lead, careers,
Hovers bewildered, and, crumpling up its wings,
Plummets to earth, to lie upon the dust
A bleeding thing, suffused with anguish, broken.
At last she gathered the remnants of her strength;
Huddling within her corner, stoic, cold,
And burying her head within her cowl,
She parried all the gimlet eyes that strove
To penetrate the shadows to her mood.
And when the curé lifted up his hands
And blessed his flock, the derelict went shuffling
Along the aisle and vanished in the mist
Of Lac la Croix.

        Some untoward circumstance
Stifled my breath—perhaps the atmosphere,
The fetid body-odors in the room.

I hurried from the hall to sun-washed air.
Bridling my sorrel mare, I found the trail
That skirts the mossy banks of Stonybrook,
And cantered homeward to all the kindred-folk
That ever wait my coming with high heart:
My setter bitch asprawl beside the door,
Drowsy, at peace with all the droning flies;
The woodchucks, quizzical and palpitant,
That venture from their den among the logs
To query me for crumbs; the crippled doe,
Who, lodging with me, crops my meadow-grass
And tramples havoc in my bed of beets,
Gloriously confident that I shall never
Muster the will to serve her with a notice—
To all that blessed wildwood company
With whom I band myself against the world
And all its high concerns and tribulations.

Somehow the valley was uncommonly
Serene and lovely, following the rain,
The mellow benediction of the sun.
The beaver-ponds that held upon their glass
The clean clear blue of noon, the pebbly brook
Meandering its twisted silver rope
Through hemlock arches, loitering in pools
Clear-hued as brimming morning-glories, placid,
Save when a trout would put a slow round kiss
Upon the water—these were beautiful.
The rustle of winds among the aspen-trees,
The fragrance on the air when my sorrel mount,
Loping upon the trail, flung down her hoofs

Upon the wintergreen and left it bruised
And dripping—these were very clean and cool.
And I was glad for the wild plums crimsoning
Among the leaves, and for the frail blue millers
Glinting above them—chips of a splintered sky;
Glad for the blossoming alfalfa fields
Robust with wining sap, and the asters bobbing
And chuckling at the whimsies of the breeze;
Glad for the far jang-jangling cattle-bells
That intimated a land of deep wet grass
And lazy water, a world of no distress,
No pain, no sorrow, a valley of contentment.

Until I came upon a mullein stalk,
Withered and bended almost to the ground
Beneath the weight of a raucous purple grackle—
A weed so scrawny of twig, so gnarled, so old,
That when I flung a pebble at the bird
Heavy upon the bough, and the purple bird
Soared singing into heaven, the mullein failed
To spring its ragged blades from earth again—
The suppleness of life had gone from it.
Something in this distressed me, haunted me.
Something in mullein, stricken, drooping, doomed—
When I can hear the rustle of a ghost
Upon November wind, a ghost that whispers
Of chill white nights and brittle stars to come,
Of solitude with never a creature sounding,
Save lowing moose, bewildered by the snow,
Forlornly rumped against the howling wind—
Something in palsied mullein troubles me.

PART V

SPLIT-RAIL FENCES

CATTLE BELLS

How clear tonight the far jang-jangling bells
Of Champlain's herd, the melody that wells
Tuneful as stony water, from the nook
   In the sweet-grass marsh of Alder Brook.

What patient strength of earth their tones disclose:
The peace of stars like quiet-falling snows,
Of forests slumbering, soundless, but for the fox
   Stepping among the clinking rocks.

What world unsullied, free of guile and snare,
What valley of contentment they declare:
A valley soothing as its bullfrog croak,
   Serene as the one slim drifting smoke;

A valley of waters that softly talk of dreams,
Of the slow sweet enterprises of little streams,
Of their solemn concern with every woodland thing
   Lingering to bathe a paw, a wing;

Of the veery, thick with sleep, who stretched his throat
And tossed in the brook a single pebbly note;
Of the frothing doe who buried her muzzle, drank,
   And dropped in the brookmints on the bank. . . .

I shall lie down and sleep . . . sleep now . . .
And yield to the cool bells this blazing brow—
Knowing grief will not stalk me, nor intrude
   Longer tonight upon my brood.

Now that the placid bells have given birth
To the gentle certainties of night and earth,
I shall lie down and sleep, sleep tranquilly;
And trouble, trouble will fall from me.

HOLLYHOCKS

I have a garden, but, oh, dear me!
What a ribald and hysterical company:
Incorrigible mustard, militant corn,
Frivolous lettuce, and celery forlorn;
Beets apoplectic and fatuous potatoes,
Voluptuous pumpkins and palpitant tomatoes;
Philandering pickles trysting at the gate,
Onions acrimonious, and peppers irate;
And a regiment of hollyhocks marching around them
To curb their mischief, to discipline and bound them.

Hollyhocks! Hollyhocks! What should I do
Without the morale of a troop like you!

Some lackadaisically yawn and nod;
Others, hypochondriac, droop on the sod:
Cabbage apathetic, parsnips sullen,
Peas downtrodden by the lancing mullein;
Boorish rutabagas, dill exotic,
The wan wax-bean, bilious and neurotic;
Dropsical melons, varicose chard,
And cauliflowers fainting all over the yard.
Thank heaven for the hollyhocks! Till day is done
They prod them to labor in the rain and the sun.

Hollyhocks! Hollyhocks! Stiff as starch!
Fix your bayonets! Forward! March!

TOBY GOES TO MARKET

We shipped the calf to the market—
    Toby, the brindle-bull,
With his face of perpetual wonder,
    And his tail like stuck-out wool.

Toby, who wallowed in mischief:
    Who squirmed through the pasture-rails,
Trampled my garden of melons,
    Battered my milking-pails.

Toby, who cried in the downpour,
    Too frugal of brindle brain
To dash from the storm into shelter,
    Or rump himself to the rain.

We tried to corral him for market;
    He blatted, his fear intense,
Straddled his legs on a railing,
    And hung himself on the fence.

We cornered him and roped him,
    He flung out his legs and sprawled;
We dragged him into the cow-pen,
    And there bewildered he bawled.

I drove him into the runway
    That leads to the cattle-cars;
He rattled his heels on the pickets
    And battered his head on the bars.

Pierre jammed him in with the cattle,
  Beside his bellowing cow;
She lowed to her suckling gently
  And licked the blood from his brow.

And Toby trembled beside her,
  Fear in his big brown eyes,
As he heard the thunder and tumult
  Of clamoring cattle rise.

A lurch of the snorting engine
  Flung him beneath the feet
Of steers that trampled him earthward;
  And Toby began to bleat.

He was on his way to the market,
  Toby, the neighborhood pet,
Who had licked the salt from my fingers
  And slavered my hands with wet.

He was off on the big adventure;
  He was reluctant to go
On a jaunt that had no returning—
  Oh, Toby, how did you know!

APRIL, WHAT WONDER-WORKING

April, what wonder-working beauty in your hand!—
That cups the world this day as craftily
As my five winnowing fingers hold
This lump of drab wet sand
And change it into thin-blown swirling gold
By magic of my breath, the sea
Spangling a foam on it, the sun
Glinting its liquid yellow on the dun.

Your mellow showers that start the cherry's blood
Bounding to every beauty-swollen bud,
Until the petals swarm and swim
Like crimson millers on the cherry limb;
Your breath, so fragrant with wet loam, so cool,
That bends the anemones and billows
The dripping green of ferns and willows
Into each woodland pool;
Your rattling rains that drum
Alert the companies of wild goose-plum—
These quicken the once dead earth,
Call up the miracle of glad new birth,
And conjure the colors of a lovely dream to come.

Hold me, O April, with your cool blue-fingered rain,
And wash me free of winter-bitterness and pain;
Renew me, April, root and stalk and leaf,
As any budding bough or blossoming sheaf.

IMPASSE

Six little sheep
Bleating in the sun,
Don't know which
Way they should run.

Fence to the left;
Fence to the right;
Before them a mouse
Stabs them with fright.

Nothing to do
But to wheel and go—
A little too much
For sheep to know.

WINTER NIGHT

O

ZERO

Zero the thread of quicksilver;
  Zero the hour of sleep;
And zero my dreams as I number
  And herd my galloping sheep.

I

BRITTLE WORLD

Brittle the snow on the gables,
  The sleet-hung pines, the night
Sprinkled with stars that quiver
  Over the waste of white.

Fragile the earth in the moonlight,
  The glassy sheet of lake;
If I tapped it with a hammer,
  The brittle world would break.

II

MY NEIGHBOR TREMPLEAU

The brood of my neighbor Trempleau
  In the cabin across the glen,
Has huddled itself in slumber
  Like woodchucks in a den.

His wife no doubt in the attic,
  Beside her whimpering drove;

Old Antoine sprawled on the sofa;
    The cat by the kitchen-stove.

There's a light in the parlor window . . .
    Felice in the feather-bed
Tossing through night with her fever,
    A crucifix at her head.

III

SKULKING BLUE

What's that!—above the rafter! . . .
    What shuffle of ghostly feet!—
There!—by the frosted window! . . .
    Only the crackle of sleet.

And that!—from the deep of the forest—
    That mournful quavering wail
With its river of icy bugling! . . .
    Ah, Trempleau's dog on a trail.

What troubles the hound in the moonlight? . . .
    A bobcat hovering near?
A rabbit among the cedars?
    The scent of a floundering deer?

Or is it the ghost of a shadow,
    The Skulking Blue in the pines
That only a dog in the moonlight
    Mysteriously divines?

THE LAMPS OF BRACKEN-TOWN

Beneath a canopy of ferns
The frosted berries hung;
Like lanterns on a slender arm,
Their blazing crimson swung—
Lanterns to rout the brooding dark,
To blaze the way of crickets
Adventuring down the gloomy streets
Beneath the bracken-thickets.

A DOG'S LIFE

To Horsford Ben Field
A Springer Spaniel

Such captivating quantities of dirt
   For a little dog to dig each day;
But, oh, how enormous the expanse of earth!—
   And China is so far away.

So numerous the beautiful bare bones
   To bury furtively in the soil—
And quickly forget! What desperate search for them!
   What furious futile toil!

(Heaven help the wretch who invented bones that need
   Bedding in some secluded place,
And cursed all little dogs with memories
   For only their master's face.)

So many lamps that bewilderingly crash
   Down from the table and on the floor;
So many scurrilous jeering brooms that sweep
   You cowering out the door.

So many nights of whimpering in the rain—
   Scolded, ejected, cuffed. And for what?
A ravaged boot and on the living-room rug
   A whimsically dribbled spot.

(Indeed, when a spaniel nips at the cook's legs,
   Trips her flat feet, and chews her stocking—

What is the flagrant crime in this droll game?
    What can there be so shocking?—

What is a pantaloon, one more, one less,
    To the granite limbs of such a slattern!
And her legs are intact—thank God!—and the pool on the rug
    Left such a lovely pattern!)

Oh, the life of a little dog is a dog's life,
    My dear, dejected, blundering Benny!
Your days are so full of solemn affairs,
    Your troubles so dismal, so many.

Small wonder that you sprawl by the fire at night,
    Wearily sigh, and close your eyes,
To dream, with scarcely a whimper or a moan,
    Of a spaniel paradise;

Of a country of no suavely arrogant cats
    Strutting in lamp-littered living-rooms,
A region of no black pills to gulp, no skunks,
    No cooks—praise God!—no brooms.

WHEN THE ROUND BUDS BRIM

When April showers stain
The hills with mellow rain,
The quaking aspen tree,
So delicate, so slim,
In glittering wet festoons,
Is a lovely thing to see—
When the round buds brim
And burst their fat cocoons,
Like caterpillars, clean,
And cool, and silver-green,
Uncurling on the limb.

And lovely when September,
With magic pigment dyes
The aspen stems with wings
Of flimsy butterflies—
When the frosted leaf swings
Its gold against the sun
And dances on the bough.

But when in bleak November
The latest web is spun,
And the gold has turned to dun—
When winds of winter call
And the bare tree answers
As the last leaves fall
Like crumpled moths—oh, now
How sad it is to look

Upon the leaves in the brook—
So many tattered hosts,
So many haggard ghosts,
So many broken dancers.

WIND IN THE PINE

Oh, I can hear you, God, above the cry
Of the tossing trees—
Rolling your windy tides across the sky,
And splashing your silver seas
Over the pine,
To the water-line
Of the moon.
Oh, I can hear you, God,
Above the wail of the lonely loon—
When the pine-tops pitch and nod—
Chanting your melodies
Of ghostly waterfalls and avalanches,
Washing your wind among the branches
To make them pure and white.

Wash over me, God, with your piney breeze,
And your moon's wet-silver pool;
Wash over me, God, with your wind and night,
And leave me clean and cool.

WHOOPING CRANE

Oh, what a night it was for dreams:
  The bayou placid after rain;
The pensive moon, the silver gleams—
  And among the reeds, a crane.

Like a silver fountain fixed by frost,
  All night the stilted sleeping bird
In frozen winter-sleep was lost;
  Never a feather stirred.

OCTOBER SNOW

Swiftly the blizzard stretched a frozen arm
    From out the hollow night—
Stripping the world of all her scarlet pomp,
    And muffling her in white.

Dead white the hills; dead white the soundless plain;
    Dead white the blizzard's breath—
Heavy with hoar that touched each woodland thing
    With a white and silent death.

In inky stupor, along the drifted snow,
    The sluggish river rolled—
A numb black snake caught lingering in the sun
    By autumn's sudden cold.

MONGREL

O mongrel, what cold brute-circumstance gave birth
To your deformity: your head low-hung,
Your mangled tail that droops upon the earth,
Your rump so battle-scarred and under-slung?

What beats your spirit down forlorn and numb?
The needles of rain upon your ribs? the sleet
Pelting your belly like pebbles on a drum?
Or the cannonade of hostile passing feet?

Yours is a desolate world, O cringing hound:
A world of so many gamins, so many stones;
Of so many garbage-cans that reward your round
Of them each day with so many barren bones.

And yours a frustrate prospect: so many heels
To scurry after in the milling throng—
Promising man-smells that draw your dumb appeals—
And never a smell to which you may belong.

Creep closer, gutter-waif. Why shrink from me,
From my amiable hand, as from a blow?
Why cower at my glance and timorously
Search in my face for sign of friend or foe?

Ah, this is better—so! the yielding eyes,
The black wet nose that nuzzles in my palm,
The paw that seeks to rest upon my thighs,
The ecstatic blur of tail! . . . and now such calm!

Why must the world forever be a boot
To you, a hobnailed boot with iron tread,
That ever falls afoul of you, poor brute,
And plants its sentiments upon your head?

Oh, yours the guilt of having dam and sire,
Sloven of breed, conceive a loathsome brat
Out of their furtive moment of desire,
A son with blood-line neither this nor that.

Your sole offense is that you once were born,
Sprung from a scabrous ill-begotten pair;
For this the world will stone you low with scorn
And slam its doors against you everywhere.

Your blood shall wash your forebears clean, your pain
Atone their sins—sins visited on you;
Thus did my pharisaic fathers ordain
Of men and magdalens, of mongrels, too.

O foundling, when dancers dance and fiddlers play,
Why must the Fiddler tax the sons of the dancers?
I ask my neighbors: Why must the mongrels pay?
But nobody listens, nobody, nobody answers.

OLD OAK

Oh, you and I, old oak, beneath the leaden skies
  Of waning autumn, shall hold our ways together;
For the hermit-thrush departs, and our fickle summer flies
  Before the hoary breath of sterner weather.

Old oak forlorn and mournful, together we shall know
  A calm white death—the cold moon riding by,
The silent winter-sleep beneath the soundless snow,
  The still companionship of starry sky.

O mournful tree, why yearn with suppliant arms to hold
  The migrant bird? Why weep with windy grief?
Why cling with great gaunt hands to the hollow charms, the
    cold
  And faded love of the last palsied leaf?

Mourn not; for we shall know again the summer sun,
  New greener leaves, the vagrant bird, and the gleams
Of bees that nuzzle the buds when the rains of April run.
  Grieve not; for now is the time for quiet dreams.

STRANGE HARVEST

Twenty-four corn-stalks yearly I grow,
Like tilted telephone-poles in a row;
What profit they earn, in what they excel,
Nobody knows, nobody can tell.

Always the talons of an August frost
Strangle my corn and my crop is lost,
When the young green ears are scarcely in silk—
Oh, long before the kernels hold milk.

My plums are as many as the leaves that flutter;
My pumpkins as pretty as a tub of butter;
My beets so sturdy they can almost walk;
But never a corn-cob sags on a stalk.

Each May when I sow my handful of grain,
My neighbor, Jeremy, divinely profane,
Flapping his arms till his face grows red,
Wrangles with me as he wags his head:

"Those whole damn' parish, she think—me, too!—
There's something the matter she is wrong with you!
Ain't never no habitant in Gasconade
Harvest an ear from those green-corn blade."

But I whistle and I plant my profitless crop
While the jaws of Jeremy open and drop—
Secure in the knowledge that my grains will earn
A more or less fickle but rich return.

In autumn, when the full brown breast of my field
Bulges the cheeks of my barn with its yield,
I reap their harvest—when the rude winds justle
The slim yellow blades and the corn-stalks rustle.

Hour upon hour, when the world is forlorn,
I perch on a stump by the sheaves of my corn
That stretch like fiddle-strings across the breeze
And I gather a beauty that no man sees.

October, scraping the bow of her wind,
Moody, torrential, undisciplined,
Saws on the dry yellow stalks and wrings
A hundred tunes from the corn-blade strings:

Mad strains that set my sun-spangled oaks
To dancing and swirling their crimson cloaks,
Like gypsies bouncing their hips on the green
To the jingling pennies in a tambourine;

A dirge for the last bronze leaf in November;
Requiems for snow to fall in December;
Lullabies, seven, for the hibernating peepers,
The chipmunk, the bear—for all the Seven Sleepers.

And there are days when they crackle like antennae
Of a radio, and their functions are many—
Blustery days in autumn when I use
My whistling corn to comb the wind for news:

News of Manitoba and her night's raw breath
Scourging the maples to a scarlet death;

Of wing-weary geese, like arrows from a quiver,
Whistling down the moonlit lane of Rouge River;

News of Indian summer, momentary, sweet,
And pungent as the taste of black-walnut meat;
Of Aurora Borealis bridging Alaska,
Of caribou rumped to the storms of Athabasca.

My stalks inform me when to chink my walls
And to bed my cattle in their snug-built stalls;
Of the day to take my sacks to the cranberry-bogs,
And the week to split maple for my fireplace logs.

Oh, I lean on my corn, with adequate reason;
It prophesies the weather, the moods of each season,
More certainly than pages from an almanac
And the disemboweled genius of the zodiac.

But sometimes I wonder if my neighbor's fear
Is the flowering of truth, if I am a bit queer;
And guiltily I turn to the solemn affairs
Of feeding my swine and currying my mares.

And Jeremy, pausing on his way to town,
Yields me a smile for the customary frown;
"Bonjour, mon fils!" he cries while his knuckles
Whimsically sink in my ribs and he chuckles.

"Now you show-it brains!—don't rattle like peas!
You always had-it ears for those coming freeze;
You got-it sharp eye for those weather and those soil—
Ain't much of your crop catch-it frost and spoil.

"Those magic is puzzlement to me! You're smart!
Also you're owning stout arm, stout heart.
If you keep from those corn, you'll be—sacré!—
The best damn' settler in the parish Beaupré."

THE FOG-BELL

All the long night, all the long day,
  When the thick gray fogs of the sea were rolling,
Where combers boom in the leaden gloom
  I heard the lugubrious fog-bell tolling.

All the long night, all the long day,
  With a sullen song and a voice grown weary,
The slow-tongued bell at each long low swell
  Complained of a life abysmally dreary.

All the long night, all the long day,
  Rest from the tides! was the theme of her moaning;
But the thin-lipped surge, a pitiless urge,
  Cracked his white lash and jeered at her groaning.

THE DEER HUNT

Oh, what a tale these rambling buck-tracks scrawl,
Bateese, upon the pages of the earth;
There seems to be no end to it, unless
We stalk him and take the story in our hands . . .

He's a king buck, Bateese. Look!—these pointed hoofs,
Split and spread out, as big as any elk's;
The rack of antlers that crowns his tossing head
Twists like a gnarled oak bough against the sky . . .

Look!—at these upturned leaves: he pawed the snow
And glared at a rival buck that blocked his way;
He's at the height of the rutting season, roaming,
Looking for something, somebody—someone lovely . . .

What a tangled skein of tracks in this blue thicket . . .
Last night he nibbled the buds of yonder birch,
Browsed on these tender poplar twigs . . . and look!—
Sprung from her bed on the snowy moss—a doe!

The prints of a doe!—so delicate, slender, sharp . . .
Scampering at her heels a playful fawn . . .
The buck-tracks cover hers; he nosed the soil,
Sniffed at her musk, and bounded after her . . .

And there—see, Bateese?—there in the ferny hollow,
He caught and covered the doe—last night—when the moon
Silvered the firs; and they dropped down together
To rest, to nose one another, to nip at the fawn . . .

Here!—on the bluff—this whirlpool of melting hoof-prints,
These droppings, four hours old: they stood at sun-up
Watching the apple-green and pink of dawn,
The slim blue smoke of the cabin down in the valley . . .

And now he's running alone, and rutting again . . .
These paws!—a hound's on his trail!—with one bad toe—
Charbonneau's mongrel! . . . Here on the hill the buck
Paused for a moment, winded the bitch, and bolted.

What a beautiful run! Twenty-four feet at a jump!
There's a bundle of clock-springs in every sinewy leg.
And he's wary, Bateese; he doubled back on his trail,
Buried his tracks in this brook, and befuddled the hound . . .

Poor brute! He's weary and hot; there at the foot
Of the mossy boulder he buried his foaming nose
In the icy spring and down his burning throat
Rippled great globes of water . . . and loped along . . .

Here, on the thickety ridge that sheltered him
From the wind, he bedded himself for a fleeting sleep—
See? where his warm flesh matted the snow and moss—
Facing his back-track, to guard against hounds and wolves.

And here he rested until—*we've jumped him, Bateese!*
He winded our taint—and look! a thirty-foot leap!
Over the basswood windfall . . . Steady! . . . Sh-sh-sh! . . .
Steady! . . . Now sneak! . . . Slow! . . . Sneak! . . .
    Slow! . . .

Sh-sh-sh! . . . Bateese!—yonder among the birches!—
Beautiful! Posing—copper against the vermilion—

III

That high-flung head indifferent to the snow
Showering upon it from the crusted branches.

Those antlers—sixteen gnarly points, or more:
Eight Aprils of browsing on tender maple buds;
Eight Augusts of idling in cool wet ferns at noon;
Eight autumns of nuzzling does among the hemlocks . . .

Sh-sh-sh! Don't move! He's tilting up his muzzle,
Trying to catch our wind again and place us—
His nostrils are quivering like poplar-leaves,
His muscles rippling like water in a brook.

What eyes, Bateese!—melting, huge, suffused—
One moment mellow brown, abrim with fear,
Another terribly alive with anger,
Blazing like rubies in a pool of fire . . .

Why don't I let him have it? I—I can't!
He reminds me of someone, something—I can't say what;
Why don't I draw my bead upon the moon!
Or murder a wood-thrush caroling at twilight! . . .

You shoot! . . . Your face is white! Your hand—your rifle—
Palsied, and wavering crazily! . . . Buck-fever!
Buck-fever, sure enough! . . . You can't shake it off!
You can't shake it off, I tell you! You can't! You can't! . . .

What a blast! . . . He's down! and writhing! He's up again!
Tottering, stunned . . . He's down! . . . And up again!
Stamping! You creased his haunch—a nick!—He's off!
Showing his rump to you—and snorting farewell.

LOOK FOR ME

When the sinking sun
Goes down to the sea,
And the last day is done,
Oh, look for me
Beneath no shimmering monument,
Nor tablet eloquent
With a stiff decorous eulogy;
Nor yet in the gloom
Of a chipped and chiseled tomb.

But when the pregnant bud shall burst
With April's sun, and bloom
Upon the bough—
Look for me now,
In the sap of the first
Puccoon whose fragile root,
Bruised by the rain,
Has left a crimson stain
Upon the cedar-glade.

Oh, look for me then,
For I shall come again,
In the leopard-lily's shoot,
And in the green wet blade
Of the peppergrass.
When the warm winds pass
Over the waking rills,
And the wild arbutus spills
Its fragrance on the air—

Look for me then—
Asleep in a ferny glen
High in the hills,
Deep in the dew-drenched maiden-hair;
I shall be waiting, waiting there.

PART VI

FLYING MOCCASINS

THE SQUAW-DANCE *

Beat, beat, beat, beat, beat upon the tom-tom,
Beat, beat, beat, beat, beat upon the drum.
Hóy-eeeeeee-yáh! Hóy-eeeeeee-yáh!
Shuffle to the left, shuffle to the left,
Shuffle, shuffle, shuffle to the left, to the left.
Fat squaws, lean squaws, gliding in a row,
Grunting, wheezing, laughing as they go;
Bouncing up with a scuffle and a twirl,
Flouncing petticoat and hair in a whirl.
Rheumatic hags of gristle and brawn,
Rolling in like a ponderous billow;
Fair squaws lithe as the leaping fawn,
Swaying with the wind and bending with the willow;
Bouncing buttock and shriveled shank,
Scuffling to the drumbeat, rank on rank;
Stolid eye and laughing lip,
Buxom bosom and jiggling hip,
Weaving in and weaving out,
Hí! Hi! Hí! with a laugh and a shout,
To the beat, beat, beat, beat, beat upon the tom-tom,
Beat, beat, beat, beat, beat upon the drum;
Hóy-eeeeeee-yáh! Hóy-eeeeeee-yáh!
Hí! Hi! Hí! Hi! Hóy-eeeeeeeeeeeeee-yáh!

Medicine-men on the medicine-drum,
Beating out the rhythm—here they come!
Medicine-gourd with its rattle, rattle, rattle,

* See *Appendix*, page 335, for supplementary comments concerning "The Squaw-Dance" and other poems in this group, Part VI.

Flinging wild with the call of battle.
Beaded drummers squatting in the ring
Leap to its challenge with a crouch and a spring;
Weathered old bucks who grunt and wheeze
As they jangle bells on their wrists and their knees:
Shining new and olden bells,
Silver, copper, golden bells,
Cow-bells, toy bells, ringing sleigh-bells,
Beaded dance bells, "give-away" bells,
Jingling, jangling, jingling bells,
Set-the-toes-atingling bells—
To the beat, beat, beat, beat, beat upon the tom-tom,
Beat, beat, beat, beat, beat upon the drum;
Hóy-eeeeeee-yáh! Hóy-eeeeeee-yáh!
Hí! Hi! Hí! Hi! Hóy-eeeeeeeeeeeeee-yáh!

Old bucks stamping heel and toe,
Ugh! as they snort and they cackle and they crow;
Yowling like the lynx that crouches nigh,
Howling like the wolf at the prairie sky;
Growling and grunting as they shift and they tramp,
Stalking, crouching—with a stamp, stamp, stamp—
Sleek limbs, lithe limbs, strong and clean limbs,
Withered limbs, bowed limbs, long and lean limbs;
Flat feet, bare feet, dancing feet,
Buckskin-moccasined prancing feet,
Eager child-feet, scuffling feet,
Feet, feet, feet, feet, shuffling feet!
Hi! Beat, beat, beat, beat, beat upon the tom-tom,
Beat, beat, beat, beat, beat upon the drum;
Shuffle to the left, shuffle to the left,

Shuffle, shuffle, shuffle to the left, to the left—
Hí! Hi! Hí! Hi! Hóy-eeeeeeeeeeeeee-yáh!

"I have a pretty present for Mah-éen-gans,
For 'Little-Wolf' I have a pretty medicine-bag.
Broidered upon it are many little beads
In many pretty patterns of wild lilies—
Yellow beads and beads of the color of the cornflower.
Through the many winter moons
I labored on this gift of friendship;
In this gaily patterned medicine-bag
I left my weary eyes and my worn fingers.
Now I wish 'the Wolf' to dance with me in the ring.
Hi! Beat, beat upon the drums, old medicine-men!
Dance! Dance in the ring, my people, and sing!"

Ho! Hó! Ho! Hó!
Hi-yáh! Hi-yáh!

Hóy-eeeeeeeee-yáh! Hóy-eeeeeeeee-yáh!
Hí! Hi! Hí! Hi! Hóy-eeeeeeeeee-yáh!
Beat, beat, beat, beat, beat upon the tom-tom,
Beat, beat, beat, beat, beat upon the drum,
As a bouncing breast and a lean long thigh,
Caper to the ring with a whoop and a cry,
And shuffle to the left, shuffle to the left,
Shuffle, shuffle, shuffle to the left, to the left—
Hí! Hi! Hí! Hi! Hóy-eeeeeeeeee-yáh!

119

"I have a present for the 'Wind-Woman,'
A present equal in value to her medicine-bag.
Ho! A pretty present, a mí-gis chain
Of many little mí-gis shells—
As beautiful as the 'North-Wind-Woman.'
My chain of shells will shake
And shimmer on her breast
As the silver brooks that tinkle
Down the moonlit bosom of yonder mountain.
Now I wish the woman to dance with me in the ring.
Hi! Beat, beat upon the drums, old medicine-men!
Dance! Dance in the ring, my people, and sing!"

Ho! Hó! Ho! Hó!
Hi-yáh! Hi-yáh!

Hóy-eeeeeeeeeeee-yáh! Hóy-eeeeeeeeeeee-yáh!
Hí! Hi! Hí! Hi! Hóy-eeeeeeeeeeeeeeeeee-yáh!
Beat, beat, beat, beat, beat upon the tom-tom,
Beat, beat, beat, beat, beat upon the drum.
Medicine-gourd with its rattle, rattle, rattle,
Ringing wild with the call of battle.
Rheumatic hags of gristle and brawn,
Rolling in like a ponderous billow;
Fair squaws lithe as the leaping fawn,
Swaying with the wind and bending with the willow.
Bouncing buttock and shriveled shank,
Scuffling to the drumbeat, rank on rank.
Old bucks stamping heel and toe,

Ugh! as they snort and they cackle and they crow—
Sleek limbs, lithe limbs, strong and clean limbs,
Withered limbs, bowed limbs, long and lean limbs;
Flat feet, bare feet, dancing feet,
Buckskin-moccasined prancing feet;
Shuffle to the left, shuffle to the left,
Shuffle, shuffle, shuffle to the left, to the left;
With a crouch and a spring and a grunt and a wheeze,
And a clanging of bells at the wrists and the knees:
Shining new and olden bells,
Silver, copper, golden bells—
Feet, feet, feet, feet, scuffling feet!
To the drumbeat, drumbeat, beat, beat, beat—
Hí! Hi! Hí! Hi! Hóy-eeeeeeeee-yáh!

THE BLUE DUCK *

Hí! Hi! Hí! Hi!
Hí! Hi! Hí! Hi!
Kéetch-ie Má-ni-dó, Má-ni-dó,
The hunter-moon is chipping,
Chipping at his flints,
At his dripping bloody flints.
He is rising for the hunt,
And his face is red with blood
From the spears of many spruces,
And his blood is on the leaves
That flutter down.
The Winter-Maker, white Bee-bóan,
Is walking in the sky,
And his windy blanket
Rustles in the trees.
He is blazing out the trail
Through the fields of nodding rice
For the swift and whistling wings
Of his She-shé-be,
For the worn and weary wings
Of many duck—
Ho! Plenty duck! Plenty duck!
Ho! Plenty, plenty duck!

Hí! Hi! Hí! Hi!
Hí! Hi! Hí! Hi!
Kéetch-ie Má-ni-dó, Má-ni-dó,

* See *Appendix*, page 338, for supplementary comments concerning "The Blue Duck" and other poems in this group, Part VI.

The seasons have been barren.
In the Moon-of-Sugar-Making,
And the Moon-of-Flowers-and-Grass,
From the blighted berry patches
And the maple-sugar bush,
The hands of all my children
Came home empty, came home clean.
The big rain of Nee-bín, the Summer-Maker,
Washed away the many little partridge.
And good Ad-ík-kum-áig, sweet whitefish,
Went sulking all the summer-moons,
Hiding in the deepest waters,
Silver belly in the mud,
And he would not walk into my nets! Ugh!
Thus the skin-sacks and the mó-kuks
Hang within my wéeg-i-wam empty.

Soon the winter moon will come,
Slipping through the silent timber,
Walking on the silent snow,
Stalking on the frozen lake.
Lean-bellied,
Squatting with his rump upon the ice,
The phantom wolf will fling
His wailings to the stars.
Then Wéen-di-gó, the Devil-Spirit,
Whining through the lodge-poles,
Will clutch and shake my teepee,
Calling,
Calling,
Calling as he sifts into my lodge;

And ghostly little shadow-arms
Will float out through
The smoke-hole in the night—
Leaping, tossing shadow-arms,
Little arms of little children,
Hungry hands of shadow-arms,
Clutching,
Clutching,
Clutching at the breast that is not there . . .
Shadow-arms and shadow breasts . . .
Twisting,
Twisting,
Twisting in and twisting out
On the ghostly clouds of smoke . . .
Riding on the whistling wind . . .
Riding on the whistling wind . . .
Riding on the whistling wind . . .
Starward! . . .
Blow, blow, blow Kee-wáy-din, North Wind,
Warm and gentle on my children,
Cold and swift upon the wild She-shé-be,
Ha-a-ah-ee-ooo! . . . Plenty duck . . .
Ha-a-a-a-ah-eeee-ooooo! . . . Plenty duck. . . .

Hí! Hi! Hí! Hi!
Hí! Hi! Hí! Hi!
Kéetch-ie Má-ni-dó, Má-ni-dó,
Blow on Áh-bi-tóo-bi many wings;
Wings of teal and wings of mallard,
Wings of green and blue.
My little lake lies waiting,

Singing for her blustery lover;
Dancing on the golden-stranded shore
With many little moccasins,
Pretty little moccasins,
Beaded with her silver sands,
And with her golden pebbles.
And upon her gentle bosom
Lies mah-nó-min, sweetest wild rice,
Green and yellow,
Rustling blade and rippling blossom—
Hi-yee! Hi-yee! Blow on Áh-bi-tóo-bi plenty duck!
Ho! Plenty, plenty duck!
Ho! Plenty duck, plenty duck!
Ho! Ho!

Hí! Hi! Hí! Hi!
Hí! Hi! Hí! Hi!
Kéetch-ie Má-ni-dó, Má-ni-dó,
I place this pretty duck upon your hand;
Upon its sunny palm and in its windy fingers.
Hi-yeee! Blue and beautiful
Is he, beautifully blue!
Carved from sleeping cedar
When the stars like silver fishes
Were aquiver in the rivers of the sky;
Carved from dripping cedar
When the Kóo-koo-kóo dashed hooting
At the furtive feet
That rustle in the leaves—
Hi! And seasoned many moons, many moons,
Ho! Seasoned many, many, many sleeps!

Hi-yeee! Blue and beautiful
Is he, beautifully blue!
Though his throat is choked with wood,
And he honks not on his pole,
And his wings are weak with hunger,
Yet his heart is plenty good.
Hi-yee! His heart is plenty good!
Hi-yee! Plenty good, plenty good!
Hi-yee! Hi-yee! Hi-yee! His heart is good!

My heart like his is good!

Ugh! My tongue talks straight!

Ho!

THUNDERDRUMS

I

THE DRUMMERS SING:

Beat on the buckskin, beat on the drums,
Hí! Hi! Hí! for the Thunderbird comes;
His eyes burn red with the blood of battle;
His wild wings roar in the medicine-rattle.
Thunderbird-god, while our spirits dance,
Tip with your lightning the warrior's lance;
On shafts of wind, with heads of flame,
Build for us arrows that torture and maim;
Ho! may our ironwood war-clubs crash
With a thunderbolt head and a lightning flash.
Hí! Hi! Hí! hear the Cut-throat's doom,
As our wild bells ring and our thunderdrums boom.

II

DOUBLE-BEAR DANCES

Hí! Hi! Hí
My wild feet fly,
For I follow the track
Of a cowardly pack;
Footprints here,
Footprints there—
Enemies near!—
Taint in the air!
Signs on the sod!
Ho! the Thunderbird-god

Gives me the eye
Of a hawk in the sky!—
Beat, beat on the drums,
For the Thunderbird comes.

    Ho! Ho!
    Ho! Ho!

III

BIG-SKY DANCES

Ho! hear me shout—
A Pucker-skin scout
With a nose that is keen
For winds unclean.
Look! Look! Look!
At the distant nook,
Where the hill-winds drift
As the night-fogs lift:
Ten smokes I see
Of the Cut-throat Sioux—
Ten ghosts there will be—
Ten plumes on my coup;
For my arms grow strong
With my medicine-song,
And a Pucker-skin scout
Has a heart that is stout.
Beat, beat on the drums,
For the Thunderbird comes.

    Háh-yah-ah-háy!
    Háh-yah-ah-háy!

GHOST-WOLF DANCES

Hó! Ho! Hó!
In the winds that blow
From yonder hill,
When the night is still,
What do I hear
With my Thunderbird ear?
Down from the river
A gray wolf's wail?
Coyotes that shiver
And slink the tail?
Ugh! enemies dying—
And women crying!—
For Cut-throat men—
One, two . . . nine, ten.
Hó! Ho! Hó!
The Spirit-winds blow—
Beat, beat on the drums,
For the Thunderbird comes.

Ah-hah-háy!
Ah-hah-háy!

V

IRON-WIND DANCES

Over and under
The shaking sky,
The war-drums thunder

When I dance by!
Ho! a warrior proud,
I dance on a cloud,
For my ax shall feel
The enemy reel;
My heart shall thrill
To a bloody kill—
Ten Sioux dead
Split open of head!
Look! to the West!—
The sky-line drips—
Blood from the breast!
Blood from the lips!
Ho! when I dance by,
The war-drums thunder
Over and under
The shaking sky.
Beat, beat on the drums,
For the Thunderbird comes.

Wuh!
Wuh!

VI

THE DRUMMERS SING:

Beat on the buckskin, beat on the drums,
Hí! Hi! Hí! for the Thunderbird comes;
His eyes glow red with the lust for battle,
And his wild wings roar in the medicine-rattle.
Thunderbird-god, while our spirits dance,

Tip with your lightning the warrior's lance;
On shafts of wind, with heads of flame,
Build for us arrows that torture and maim;
Ho! may our ironwood war-clubs crash
With a thunderbolt head and a lightning flash.
Hí! Hi! Hí! hear the Cut-throat's doom,
As our wild bells ring and our thunderdrums boom.

INDIAN LOVE SONG

Cold sky and frozen star
That look upon me from afar
   Know my echoed grief.

Hollow night and black butte
Hear my melancholy flute—
   Oh, sound of falling leaf.

Homeless wind and waterfall
Hold a sadness in their call,
   A sorrow I have known.

Shivering wolf and lonely loon
Cry my sorrow to the moon—
   O heavy heart . . . O stone!

INDIAN SLEEP SONG

Zhóo . . . zhoo, zhóo!
My little brown chief,
The bough of the willow
Is rocking the leaf;
The sleepy wind cries
To you, close your eyes—
O little brown chief,
Zhóo . , . zhoo, zhóo!

Kóo . . . . koo, kóo!
My little brown bird,
A wood-dove was dreaming
And suddenly stirred;
A brown mother-dove,
Dreaming of love—
O little brown bird,
Kóo . . . . koo, kóo!

Hóo . . . . hoo, hóo!
My little brown owl,
Yellow-eye frightens
Bad spirits that prowl;
For you she will keep
A watch while you sleep—
O little brown owl,
Hóo . . . . hoo, hóo!

Zhóo . . . zhoo, zhóo!
O leaf in the breeze.

Kóo . . . . koo, kóo!
Shy bird in the trees.
Sh . . . . . . sh, sh!
O snow-covered fawn.
Hóo . . . . hoo, hóo!
Sleep softly till dawn.

CRAZY-MEDICINE

Blow winds, winds blow,
North, East, South, West,
Make my foe, the cedar man,
Drunk with crazy dances;
Shake his skull until his brains
Rattle up and rattle down—
Pebbles in a gourd.

Roar winds, winds roar,
Flapping winds, jumping winds,
Winds that crush and winds that split,
Winds like copper lances;
Whistle through the crazy man,
Fling him up, fling him down—
A rag upon a cord.

Beat winds, winds beat,
Iron winds, icy winds,
Winds with hail like leaden shot
That make a sounding thunder;
Beat a sleet upon his head,
Up and down, up and down—
Hail upon a drum.

Wail winds, winds wail,
Silver winds, pointed winds,
Winds to stab a coyote soul,
In and out and under;
Send cold silver through his head,
In an ear, out an ear—
A needle through a plum.

Ai-yee! My Yellow-Bird-Woman,
My né-ne-móosh-ay, ai-yee! my Loved-One,
Be not afraid of my eyes!
Beat against me no longer!
Come! Come with a yielding of limbs!
Ai-yee! Woman, woman,
Trembling there in the teepee
Like the doe in the season of mating,
Why foolishly fearest thou me?
Cast the strange doubts from thy bosom!
Be not afraid of my eyes!
Be not as the flat-breasted squaw-sich
Who feels the first womanly yearnings
And hides, by the law of our people,
Alone three sleeps in the forest;
Be not as that brooding young woman
Who wanders forlorn in the cedars,
And slumbers with troubled dreams,
To awaken suddenly, fearing
The hot throbbing blood in her bosom,
The strange eager life in her limbs.
Ai-yee! Foolish one, woman,
Cast the strange fears from thy heart!
Wash the red shame from thy face!
Be not afraid of my glances!

Be as the young silver birch
In the Moon-of-the-Green-Growing-Flowers—
Who sings with the thrill of the sap

As it leaps to the south wind's caresses;
Who yields her rain-swollen buds
To the kiss of the sun with glad dancing.
Be as the cool tranquil moon
Who flings off her silver-blue blanket
To bare her white breast to the pine;
Who walks through the many-eyed night
In her gleaming white nudeness
With proud eyes that will not look down.
Be as the sun in her glory,
Who dances across the blue day,
And flings her red soul, fierce-burning,
Into the arms of the twilight.
Ai-yee! Foolish one, woman,
Be as the sun and the moon!
Cast the strange doubts from thy bosom!
Wash the red shame from thy face!
Thou art a woman, a woman!
Beat against me no longer!
Be not afraid of my eyes!

CHANT FOR THE MOON-OF-FREEZING

Out of my mouth, like clouds of frightened birds
That spiral up the sky before a storm,
My words go up to you, O Mystery:

Ugh! I am poor; my skin is sharp with ribs,
Flat on my belly, tight as drawn wet buckskin—
   This is very bad;
Send me a moose to kill, and make me round
With food, like a bear in the Moon-of-Falling-Leaves—
   That is very good.

Shake down good snows upon the earth, O Spirit,
Snows that are not too soft or wet for snow-shoes—
   This is very bad;
Yet brittle enough with crust to snare the legs
Of deer, and deep enough to yard the bucks—
   That is very good.

My blanket is thin and spotted with much dirt,
Like a patch of snow in spring, turned muddy, ragged—
   This is very bad;
Give me three blankets, red wool—eleven, twenty—
Better too many robes than not enough—
   That is very good.

My clothes go flapping in the wind like bark
On an old gray birch; the skinny wolf is my brother—
   This is very bad;

Give me warm shirts, vermilion—seven, ten—
And I would like a golden-measure-of-time—
      That is very good.

So much I ask, O Spirit, with a heart
That holds no bitterness. Out of my mouth
My words go up the sky like crying birds
Frightened before the sound of coming thunder.

Bronze in the rose-dusted twilight,
A statue of bronze, arms uplifted,
He stands ankle-deep in the lilies
As rigidly fixed and as silent
As a red granite butte on the prairie,
As still as the dusk in the foot-hills—
"Ho! Red-Rock, big hunter-of-moose!
Red-Rock, him fool-um old bull!
Red-Rock, big moose-killer!—Wuh!"—
Bronze in the tranquil sunset,
Statuesque bronze in the willows.

A sudden rush through the lilies;
A splashing of flashing limbs,
Shattering his mirror of silver—
Juggling his gold-glinted rainbows,
And flinging them into the winds;
A sudden swoop through the waters,
A sudden scoop of the hands—
And bronze in the copper twilight,
With arms uplifted he stands,
Statuesque bronze in the lilies—
"Red-Rock, big caller-of-moose!—Wuh!"

Dripping, dripping, dripping
Blue-shimmering drops through his fingers;
Dripping, dripping, dripping
Thin tinkling streams from his palms;
Plashing, plashing, plashing

Cupped handfuls of silvery waters
Splashing among the lilies—
Black bronze in the purple twilight,
Statuesque bronze in the night—
"Red-Rock! Big hunter-of-moose!—Wuh!"

A long low call from the valley;
A bellow, an echoing bugle
Mellow and deep with the passion
Of lone longing male for his mate:
"Hark! Hark! sweet One-in-the-Lilies!
Ho! my Splashing-One! Ho!
I come!—with my limbs aquiver!
I come!—with a straining of flanks!"

Beat-beating, beat-beating, beat-beating,
Long-loping feet in the forest;
A clashing of horn in the timber,
A crashing of hoofs in the brush . . .
A splash in the placid bayou,
An eager nose to the air,
And lo! a palpitant bellow,
A wild-ringing rapturous blare! . . .

Black bronze in the cool blue moonlight.
Black statuesque bronze in the night.
Cupped hands to the stars uplifted—
Dripping, dripping, dripping
Thin tinkling streamlets of silver,
Soft-plashing fountains of silver,
Shimmering-blue sprinklings of silver—
"Red-Rock! Big killer-of-moose!—Wuh!"

TO A DEAD PEMBINA WARRIOR

O warrior-soul, afloat
Upon the sea of night
In your ghostly birchen boat,
Anchored upon the black limb,
And etched against the white
Of the broken hunter's moon—
O spirit, dark and dim,
Draped with festoon
Of moss, and shielded by lancing pines
That ring their ragged lines
Around the somber swamp—
Sleep without fear in your birchen shroud,
Sleep with a heart secure and proud
In your ghostly burial pomp.
Know that the steadfast mountain-ash
Lifts you with mighty arms
Up to the proud flash
Of the moon, holds you high
In the unconquered sky,
Secure in a starry cache,
Safe from the harms
Of the little peoples of the earth.

Through soundless nights, with ghostly mirth,
Echoing your crimson scalping-cry
From peak to peak,
The lonely wolf will speak
Of you and your many bloody wars.
When white Bee-bóan shall heap

His snowy avalanche—
Soft as the down of the Canada goose—
In tufted drifts and bars
On the black branch
To keep you warm in winter-sleep,
The wild feet of the stars
Mirrored upon the frozen snow,
Will dance for you, row on row;
And when the hoary spruce
Bends on your head,
To whisper lullabies, to weep
Sweet songs for the dead—
Lo! out of the white deep
Of night the winter wind will sweep
Down on your birchen bed,
To wrap its arms about your clay,
To carry you away
To the land of your desires,
To the country whence you came
Like a flame,
Back to the country of your sires,
To a land of friendly council-fires.

SCALP-DANCE

Hi! Hi! Hi!

Jangle the gourds
And rumble on the drum!
Fresh from the death
Of an enemy I come,
Like a timber-wolf
Whose stomach is filled
With the heart and flesh
Of an elk he has killed.

Sound on your war-drums
Lightning and thunder,
For dancing I come
With my sacred plunder:
The scalp of Whirling-Bird,
A coward in battle—
His yellow teeth chattered
Like the stones in my rattle.

Blood on my fingers,
Blood on my lips,
Rivers of blood
From his scalp that drips
Its red like the sun
In the sinking light,
That streams its hair
Like the trailing night.

144

Blood on my battle-ax,
Blood on my lance,
Blood in the music
Of my medicine-dance;
Blood in my throat
And blood in my cry
That splinters the moon
And the bloody sky.

Hi! Hi! Hi!

PART VII

THREE WOMEN

ANGELIQUE

Twenty-one Moons-of-Berries, and Angelique,
Nurtured to ripeness in the wild black earth
Of St. Hilaire by summer suns and rains,
Waxed like a wild goose-plum upon the bough,
From brimming bud, to blossom, into fruit.
Despite the frosts that life had visited
Upon her youth—her father, mother, brothers, all
Had vanished with the Sickness-on-the-lungs—
She struggled to survival into beauty.

At twenty-two she found the will to live
In a high sweet dream of loveliness to come:
A dream of home, of a swinging cradle-board
Bearing its fretful cargo from a sea
Of trouble into the port of cool sleep;
Oh, Angelique would mother anything,
A homeless cat, a dog, a broken bird.

At twenty-three the rich maturity
Of full-blown womanhood revealed itself
In every rounded line of hip and bosom,
In every limb that pulsed with ardent wine.
Upon the tree of life she hung, in reach
Of the hand of any passing harvester:
A ripe wild plum, grown full with amber sap
As thick and clear beneath the billowy skin
As a globe of pure wild honey against the sun,
So heavy with life upon the bended twig
That any breeze might shake it from the bough.

149

But breezes in the parish St. Hilaire
Were few enough, and harvesters were fewer,
What with the lumberjacks away on drives
In distant logging-camps, and the voyageurs
Trading for pelts, or out on timber-cruise.
Thus Angelique remained upon the branch,
Powdered with bloom as any untouched fruit,
Until the government dentist, Gene Magruder,
Came with the crew of federal engineers.

Magruder was a connoisseur of fruit,
Truly a horticulturist of parts—
And smooth as darkly quiet water flowing
Over a beaver-dam. Oh, he was good
To contemplate, celestial in the eyes
Of guileless Angelique, when mimicking
The moods of heroes in the cinema,
He posed for her at evening in the pines,
Bathed in a purifying flood of moonlight—
Moonlight that draped him in a spotless robe,
And put upon his pallid face the look
Of an acolyte before a glowing candle.
More beautiful he was in lonely night,
When rippling his fingers on his cedar flute,
He stirred to life within a woman's breast
A nameless poignant yearning, the wistful will
To mother something, someone—a bird, a fawn,
An acolyte before a glowing candle.
And when at last, with patch of open throat
Silverly throbbing like a mating thrush's,
He poured his torrential ardor in a song

That dripped the melancholy of his hunger—
Oh, never a thing of throbbing human flesh
Could long withstand the beat and break of it!
Never a woman but would yield a moan,
And clutching at her breast with trembling hands,
Sink down upon the earth.

                          So Angelique!—
As when a wild goose-plum, mature for harvest,
Shaken among the leaves by a flitting thrush,
Lets loose its tenuous hold upon the twig
And drops to earth, a windfall for the world.

And if a woman, lonely, heavy with seed,
And hungry for a moment of romance,
Assured of the fulfilment of a dream
Of swinging cradle-boards, and reassured
That in the Moon-of-Falling-Leaves the curé,
Father Bazile, would bind them with the banns
And sanctify their evening of delight—
If such a woman, in this circumstance
Yield to the law of gravity, what man
Of wisdom in the ways of nature will put
His heel on her, or stone her with contempt?
So Angelique!—among the grim-lipped pines
That rim the valley of the Beaverbrook . . .
While parish St. Hilaire was dark with sleep . . .
When the hollow mocking laughter of a loon
Echoed within the silver bell of night. . . .

In the Moon-of-Falling-Leaves, upon the banks
Of Beaverbrook, lone Angelique maintained

Her patient vigil, started to the door
With every coming footfall on the trail,
Caught her warm breath with every crackling twig—
As, one by one, the frosted maple-blades,
Floating their bronze upon the wistful blue
Of smoldering autumn, eddied to the sod,
Banded their warmth against a long, long snow.
When the last leaf sank, and the maple-tree was bare,
And never a thrush remained upon the bough,
Worn Angelique, grown desolate of hope,
Nursing a dream of cradle-board to come
And fearful of the thrust of village eyes,
Withdrew herself; secluded in a nook—
A cabin dark with rambling tanglewood—
Safe from the hiss and venom of village talk
That glided, snake-like, on her heels when she
Went forth in day, she gave herself to dreams,
Visions of loveliness to come, tomorrow. . . .

In St. Hilaire old Angelique abides,
Harried and bruised, a windfall for the world,
As any fallen fruit upon the ground,
Broken and pocked by the bills of many birds,
Under the foot of every passing woman,
Under the foot of every passing man.
In St. Hilaire the crone drags out her moons,
Companioned by the slender souvenir
Of a high sweet moment of romance, a seedling
Sprung from a dream gone into yesterday.
Oh, he is beautiful—in the blue of moonlight.

ALTYN, THE WORLD'S MOST WICKED CITY

Altyn, the world's most wicked city, Altyn—
All the old wranglers who jingled in the days
Of open range, and all the Vigilantes,
Cupping their palsied hands behind their ears,
Still shift reflective cuds and wag their heads
Whenever barroom talk swings around to Altyn,
The world's most wicked city.

                  Oh, sinful enough
It was when Silver Britt, of Kootenai,
Staked out his claim in Blackfoot Basin, sank
His mattock into a seam of golden luck,
And opened the Yellow Mary; when all the gates
Of hell went out and poured upon the town
A flood of rustlers, mountebanks, and harpies—
As when a logging-dam, with a mighty groan
Gives way and looses on a tranquil valley
A pent-up avalanche of rotting weeds
And slithering debris.

                  In a turbulent tide,
From every stagnant bayou of the earth
They tumbled; outlaws, renegades, and boomers,
Rakehells and courtezans and roustabouts—
The scum of every region—over the hills
They streamed, and eddied in the town of Altyn:
Alkali Brown, who ran the faro-bank
And left the miners stripped of every nugget,

With pokes as empty as a beggar's cup
Would be upon the reeling streets of Altyn;
And Kansas Kitty, vast, oleaginous,
Who amorously engulfed her maudlin guests
With ardor more fierce than Arizona noon—
The while, subtle of touch, five crooked fingers
Slipped through the sliding panel in the wall
And filched their dangling pockets; Jules Boidreau,
The Dude of Kootenai, who conjured gold-dust
Out of the money-belts of all the cruisers,
With deft white hands and the subtle abracadabra
Of walnut shells and temperamental peas.

Oh, never the tremble of a gentle tear
In the world's most wicked city; never a man
Whose heart would yield the flower of compassion.
Not even Gentleman Joe, who worked his spells
With fan-tan, chuck-a-luck, and three-card monte,
Suave as the blade of any butter-knife;
Nor even Effie Golden—she of the eyes
As wistful as a mating antelope's;
She of the lips suffused with all the warmth
Of scarlet poppies after rain; Effie,
Nobody's woman, the woman of every man;
Effie, who coiled her undulating white
Of arms about young Calvin McElroy,
Who dubbed himself a circuit-riding parson;
Effie, who breathed a passion on his mouth
That melted his will as a blow-torch melts a candle;
Effie, who poured the poison of her blood
Into his veins, and flung him out in the pink

Of morning, to stagger to his hut, shattered,
Blighted, as when a sound white apple takes
The worm from a rotten apple at its side.

Oh, desert winds fling handfuls of alkali
And dust upon the moldering bones of Altyn.
The face of Yellow Mary Mountain, pocked
By a thousand mattocks, robbed of its golden teeth,
Looks down with a crooked smile and leers at Altyn.
When the hollow moon is hooked among the pines,
The lobo, squat on a carcass, lifts his head
And quavers a melancholy requiem—
Where clanking skeletons of mining-rig
And darkly looming winch are silhouetted
Against the moon, like gibbets dangling the ghosts
Of once high dreams of Altyn.

          Nothing remains
Of the world's most wicked city; nothing remains,
Except a solitary grave that rambles
With clematis, and mallows salmon-red,
Planted by McElroy's fast-rotting fingers,
Patterned about by skulls of buffalos—
Dark-socketed tenements of drowsy bees
And darting centipedes; and girdling the mound,
Like a bulwark against the world, a wall of stone,
Painfully quarried, painfully hewn, and lifted
Painfully into place by the bleeding hands
Of rotting McElroy, the country parson;
And on the hillock, within this miniature
God's Acre, a weary weathered shingle leaning

Upon the wind, and deeply carved by hands
Palsied with fever: *Effie Golden—gone.*
Oh, nothing remains, nothing remains of Altyn,
Where never the eye of any man had known
The glint and tremble of a gentle tear;
Where never the stony furrows of a heart
Had yielded up the flower of compassion.

RATTLING-CLAW, AN INDIAN SPINSTER

For thirty Moons-of-Flowers-and-Grass she waited,
Waited for something, something that never came.
When she was but a fingerling, she took
A buckskin pack upon her shoulder-blades;
And from the cranberry swamps of Val Brillant
She slogged upon the devious snow-shoe trail
Of Two-Guns-Calf, her sire, and followed him
To Goat-haunt Range, to mountain solitude.

Ninety-four miles from kin and village folk
They lived in isolation, year on year,
Running their otter trap-lines in the hills,
Harvesting rice and roots and saskatoons,
And gathering for margin of luxury
The annual yield of fruit and maple-sugar.
Here in the hostile upland, Rattling-Claw,
Groomed by the keen wind, the alpine sun,
Waxed opulent with beauty; in maidenhood
She blossomed like a lily, a crimson lily,
Wafted as seedling from a lowland swamp
To the chilling solitude of timber-line,
And come, by stroke of chance, to rich ripe bloom—
When the mellow sun brought flushed maturity
To all her sisters in the far savanna.

I recollect the night I came on them.
The District Ranger, fearing forest-fires,
Had sent me out to run down flaming stubs
Struck in the pineries by lightning-flash.

A twilight caught me at the mountain lodge
Of Two-Guns-Calf; electing to break the night
With him, I picketed my mare, I flung
My blankets down and shared his food and flame.

While Two-Guns pried me gently for the news
Of Val Brillant, his daughter set the bowls
Of steaming wild rice, the roast of venison.
And as we spoke, she lingered at my side,
Solicitous of every mood and whim,
Trembling at every touch of a casual hand,
Eager to salvage from our talk a glance
Of admiration, a morsel of approval.

And warranted they were! Suffused her flesh
From clear cold winds; seductive was the curve
Of throat that palpitated with an ardor
Sprung from a wild sweet earth; the dusky eyes,
Low-lidded with a shy slow invitation—
A crimson lily ripe for seed, and waiting,
Waiting for pollen-bearing winds to come
From out a far low country, a humming-bird,
A butterfly, a roving honey-bee.

And later, when we left old Two-Guns nodding
Beside the fire, and ventured down the trail
To Heron Spring, to fill our birch-bark buckets—
Vivid the memory: the stoic firs,
The lichen-covered ridge, the pool of sky
Gleaming with silver pebbles, the eager pupil
Close by my side the while my finger sketched

On night the constellations, star by star—
The Northern Crown, the Bear, the Flying Swan—
Too few they were! And when a timber-wolf
Shivered the solitude with eerie wails
That drove her to my arms in playful fright:
The rounded warmth of her, the yielding flesh,
The moist vermilion of her mouth that brushed
By chance against my cheek. Oh! it would test
The iron in the will of any man
To hold secure its chill integrity
Against the surging fire of Rattling-Claw;
Either it yielded, molten, soon or late,
Or else was purified to tempered steel. . . .

In Goat-haunt Range, old Rattling-Claw, alone,
Flings out the line of traps, draws up alone
Her buckets at the spring, and sets the roast
Of venison before her palsied sire;
In Goat-haunt isolation, Rattling-Claw,
Wasted by years, by hungers unfulfilled,
Companioned by a hound on whom she rains
Her ardor, lets fall her virtues one by one
To earth like petals withered—a lily, parched
In the Moon-of-Turning-Colors-in-the-Leaves,
Raspy of blade, forlornly wilted, waiting,
Waiting for pollen-bearing winds to come
From out a far low country, a venturing moth,
A roving bee, a bird, a butterflv.

PART VIII

SADDLE-LEATHER

THE SHEEPHERDER

Loping along on the day's patrol,
I came on a herder in Madison's Hole;
Furtive of manner, blazing of eye,
He never looked up when I rode by;
But counting his fingers, fiercely intent,
Around and around his herd he went:

One sheep, two sheep, three sheep, four . . .
Twenty and thirty . . . forty more;
Strayed—nine ewes; killed—ten rams;
Seven and seventy lost little lambs.

He was the only soul I could see
On the lonely range for company—
Save a lean lone wolf and a prairie-dog,
And a myriad of ants at the foot of a log;
So I sat the herder down on a clod—
But his eyes went counting the ants in the sod:

One sheep, two sheep, three sheep, four . . .
Fifty and sixty . . . seventy more;
There's not in this flock a good bell-wether!
Then how can a herder hold it together!

Seeking to cheer him in his plight,
I flung my blankets down for the night;
But he wouldn't talk as we sat by the fire—
Corralling sheep was his sole desire;
With fingers that pointed near and far,
Mumbling, he herded star by star:

One sheep, two sheep, three—as before!
Eighty and ninety . . . a thousand more!
My lost little lambs—one thousand seven!—
Are wandering over the hills of Heaven.

BREAKERS OF BRONCOS

So! breakers of broncos! with miles of jagged wire,
You seek to break the spirit of this range;
With lariat of barbed-wire fence, you hope
To tame its heart, and with your iron heel,
Hot from the desert, to sear upon its hip
Your molten brand—as wranglers at a round-up,
With bit and spur and lasso, strive to curb
And brand an outlaw fresh from winter range.

O breakers of broncos, listen! Can't you hear
The northwind snickering at you? the coyote
Upon the mesa, jeering? the waterfall
Chuckling among the rocks? the croaking magpie,
The hooting owl, the crane, the curlew? Look!
The chokecherry blossom, the sage, the bitter-root,
Bending with mirth, wag their heads, and laugh
At you! Why, even the broomtail cayuse kicks
His heels against the mountain sky, and snorts!

O breakers of broncos, we fling you on the wind
This handful of dust, this bitter alkali!—
As well attempt to rope the bucking stars,
Or burn your bars upon the flank of the moon!
When will you whirl your lasso at the sun?
Or bridle it? or straddle the lightning-flash?

COLLOQUY WITH A COYOTE

Ki-yoo-oo-oo-oo-oo-oo!

Speak now, O coyote, rumped upon the knoll!
Into the bowl of desert night—
Clinking and cool with stars—oh, roll
The melancholy of your soul.
When sentimental with the moon, you cry
Your longing to the lady in the sky,
Know that you do not grieve for her, alone,
That your deep yearning, sprung from blight
Of solitude, is doubled by my own.
Speak then, O coyote, speak for me;
With your seductive melody cajole
The lovely one to be more intimate, invite
Her to linger for a moment of delight.
The virgin, you, and I—we three
On such a night should be more neighborly.

In the homeland whence I came, a solitude
Dark with its regiments of lancing pine
That march from peak to water-line,
I knew another spokesman for my mood—
Oh, he was suave, ingratiating, shrewd!
When balsams muffled their voices in the cowl
Of sable dusk, and tranquil, cool,
The beaver-pond was but a chip
Of silver, soundless, save for the flip
Of a beaver's tail, the flapping of an owl—

On such a night as this,
When the silver-lady put a kiss
Upon the bosom of the pool,
The gibbering loon, disconsolate, forlorn,
Flinging upon the sky a rain
Of silver tones, the tremolo of pain—
Would always gain her ear and mourn
For me, befriend me; ah, the loon
And I!—we had an understanding with the moon.

Speak then, O desert coyote, speak for me now.
Be to me kinsman in this valley of the dead,
This waste so unfamiliar, so dispirited.
Among the bleaching bones upon the brow
Of yonder butte, fling back your head,
And stabbing moonward with your wail, impart
Our sorrow till it breaks the vestal's heart;
Tell the indifferent one that she is beautiful;
As lovely and as cool
As a peeled willow bough;
Request the lady to leave off her gown
Of clouds, and ask her to come down . . .

Ki-yoo-oo-oo-oo-oo-oo!

DYNAMITE

Outlaw they brand you, killer, bucking fool,
Because you spurn the hackamore and cinch;
The round-up wranglers wait with eager heart
The moment of your fall: your steel-curbed mouth
Running a rill of blood, your back worn raw
By the saddle sticking like a cocklebur,
Your wild heart, broken by the quirt, subdued.

O bronco, whose will is set against the will
Of the multitude, as taut as any bowstring,
Know that another outcast will exult
If the free-born one shall pitch the sovereign many
Over the rim of sky and into darkness. . . .

Beware!—the burlap that they strive to fling
About your head to blind you! the velvet hands
They clamp upon your ears, your quivering mouth!
Or you will run the range tomorrow servile,
Shattered of soul as any mongrel cur.

Beware! They come! Let fly your molten heels!
Double and snort and twist! Rain down your hoofs
Of crackling thunderbolts upon the ground!
For every sweep of spur from neck to flank,
Hurtle your rider skyward, rake his head
Upon the pointed stars, and heave him sprawling
Over the moon and down to earth again.

Oh, beautiful!—the wild heart pounding, free!
The flames of hell triumphant in your eyes!

As lovely your electric flesh careering,
As the galloping cloud and lightning-flash, your kin,
The wild unfettered horses of the sky.

Well done! Well done! O bronco, run! Run!
Streaming the velvet banners of your mane,
Run free again; back to the comradeship
Of cantering rain and nickering waterfalls,
To your mountain solitude where thin blue winds
Whinny among the pines and crop the grasses.
And wait for me, O bronco, wait for me there.

DROUTH

The scorching embers of the sun
  All month had smoldered on the land,
Until the lakes and marshes, one by one,
  Were pools of glistening sand.

The pond-reeds rattled with each gasp
  Of wind like brittle yellow bones;
Endless the pessimistic cricket's rasp
  Among the crumbling stones.

The runnel, dribbling among the sheaves,
  Ran thin as a fragile silver thread,
And Shoshone River rolled a stream of leaves
  Along its blistered bed.

All day the sage, in dusty shrouds,
  Sucked at the alkali in vain;
All night the mountains combed the scudding clouds
  Desperately for rain.

SWEETWATER RANGE

I was loping along in the Sweetwater Range,
   When the shadowy clouds of sleep
On the blue earth had settled like raven's wings,
   With a swift mysterious sweep.

The valley lay calm as a beaver-pond
   When the hunter's moon hangs low,
And the hills were as soft as the velvet sod
   Under an antelope doe.

Serene overhead in the dusky blue,
   A single star through the night
Glowed like a candle held by God
   As a friendly beacon-light;

A flame in the window of His vast house,
   Beckoning out to me—
I could almost see Him peering down,
   As He waited expectantly.

So I flung Him a couple of friendly songs,
   As I cantered a lonely mile:
Swing Low, Sweet Chariot, Old Black Joe,
   Jordan, and Beautiful Isle.

For the singing of psalms my voice was raw—
   I was never a parson's pet;
And the tremolo wail of a shivering wolf
   Made it a strange duet.

But hard on the echoes—from Avalanche Peak,
  Where the Yellowrock Cataract spills—
I heard Him sing back to me clear as a bell
  In the frosty dawn of the hills.

ALKALI POOL

In the golden setting of the butte it lay,
    Deep emerald of hue;
In the copper filigree of dying day
    It gleamed a sapphire-blue.

And yet its stagnant waters held a hint
    Of alkali and lead—
And the limpid spring seemed baleful with the glint
    Of the stone in a serpent's head.

HEAVEN FOR HORSES

Shuffle along, O paint cayuse!
Prick up your flyblown ears: we've swung
The pasture-gate to turn you loose,
To let your carcass, sprained and sprung,
Your rattling bag of bones now pass
   To the paradise of grass.

Never again a pain to come
From panniers pounding on your side
Like cudgels clattering on a drum;
From saddles that gall your tender hide;
From the rake and sweep of grinding rowels
   And spurs that stab your bowels.

Time for a bronco's holiday!
Time now to watch the clouds roll by,
To nibble the knee-deep salty hay,
To roll and sprawl your heels on the sky.
O Paint-o! bed yourself in clover,
   The pull of the years is over.

Nothing to do now, but placidly stand
And wait till your sagging head shall sink;
And the ghost of you, with a flaming brand,
Will gallop over the world's brink
To heaven, with a dim white rider astraddle
   Your ribs on a ghostly saddle.

Heaven for horses!—a billowy plain
With blocks of salt in mountain-rows,

Timothy tall as pines, and grain
Foaming in oceans up to your nose;
Where a horse forever may plant his feet
  In rivers of oats and eat.

Heaven!—no starry refuge there
For the mice that worry you into flight,
Or the drolling clownish grizzly bear
Whose antics stop your heart with fright;
Nor any menacing bug or bee
  To drive you to deviltry.

What troubles you? Whoa! Why snort at this? . . .
Nothing in heaven to make you vexed!
To give you a slight excuse for the bliss
Of bucking and squealing! to serve as pretext
For bolting and running your crazy courses! . . .
  Paint! Is there a hell for horses?

Over the rim of the glacier,
Down dusk of the canyon-wall,
Like a river of sliding moonlight,
Tumbled the waterfall.

The stream of torrential moonlight
Cascaded down the blue,
Into a pool of moonlight
Among the sable yew.

Hovering above the eddies,
The fragile-pinioned foam,
Like swarms of silver millers,
Went fluttering up the gloam;

Only to perish, broken,
Shattered upon a gust
By the ponderous white of moonlight
Into a silver dust.

MOUNTAIN GOAT

Rigidly silver on the peak
  Against the sky's blue flood,
A contemplative mountain goat
  Pensively chewed his cud.

Frozen his pose, as if the wind
  Had chiseled him from snow
And sunlight had put on him a glaze
  From horn to flinty toe.

Oh, solemnly he held his eyes
  On the beauty of the plain
Outspread below him in the sun,
  Shot through with fitful rain:

The checkered April-green of field,
  The poppy's butter-gold,
The valley-mist that draped the pines
  With trembling fold on fold;

The polished turquoise of the pools
  Deep in the hills and hollows,
That mirrored the wings of flimsy clouds,
  The silken flight of swallows.

At last he wagged his wisp of beard,
  Shattered his marble mass,
Bleated a stiff sardonic "Ba-a-a!"
  And fell to munching grass.

My neighbors dubbed me a vagabond,
  A rebel, an idling clod,
Because I refused to pound my feet
On the cobblestones of a city street,
To gild my belly with wine and meat,
  To bow to their golden god.

They put me down as a ne'er-do-well,
  A shirker of sober toil,
Because I bolted their wolves' pack,
Loped a lone trail, and never turned back,
Scoffed at the game they sought to track,
  And wheeled from their paltry spoil.

They wagged their heads with concern for me;
  Sprawled by a woodland pool,
I was content at dawn to lie
And watch the triumphant eagle fly
Scrawling his freedom over the sky—
  For this they called me a fool.

God rest you content, O gentlemen!
  I break from your glittering bars,
To throb with the ultimate eagle's flight,
To know the trivial world from his height,
The wild song of the wind at night,
  And the neighborliness of stars.

Hail and farewell, you bridled all!
  When the gold of your god turns gilt,

I shall have minted the gold of the sun,
Into my arteries I shall have run
The wines of contentment, one by one,
    And never a drop shall have spilt.

And never a grace I'll ask of the world,
    Nor pity, nor earthly token;
Only a brook and a bannock-bread,
The loyal lips of the woman I wed,
And cool wet moss to pillow my head
    When my wild wings are broken.

When the passion of the day is done,
And the weary sun,
Lingering above the calm plateau
And mesa-waters, stains
The cottonwoods and sleeping cranes
With afterglow,
Day keeps a fleeting tryst
With Night in the mesa-mist.
When her crimson arm embraces
The clouds and plains
No more, spent Day slips quietly to rest
On a ghostly breast—
And nothing remains,
Save in the twilit places,
The ghosts of rains
And columbines whose wistful faces
Droop where the purple-pollened fir
Tinctures the dusk with lavender.

FISHER OF STARS

My wild blood leaped as I watched the falling stars
    Flash through the night and gleam,
Like spawning trout that hurtle the riffled bars
    Of a dusky mountain stream.

Like quivering rainbow-trout that run in spring,
    Arching the water-slides—
Out of the limpid sky, in a wild wet fling,
    They shook their crimson sides.

My sportsman's heart flamed up, as the fishes dashed
    In school on shimmering school,
Through high cascades and waterfalls, and splashed
    In the deep of a cloudy pool.

I fished that pond; I chose my longest line,
    And cast with my supplest rod—
The one was a thing of dreams, oh, gossamer-fine;
    The other a gift from God.

I flicked the Milky Way from edge to edge
    With an iridescent fly;
I whipped the polar rapids, and every ledge
    And cut-bank in the sky.

To the Pleiades I cast with my willowy pole;
    And I let my line run out
To the farthest foamy cove and skyey hole—
    And I raised a dozen trout.

And every time one struck my slender hook,
    He shattered the trembling sea,
With a sweep of his shivering silver fin, and he shook
    A silver rain on me;

My line spun out, my fly-rod bent in twain,
    As over the sky he fought;
My fingers bled, my elbows throbbed with pain—
    But my fishing went for naught.

I landed never a one; my line and hackle
    Were none too subtle and fine;
For angling stars one wants more delicate tackle—
    A more cunning hand than mine.

KOOTENAI POOL

Like clear green wine, the water in the pool,
In a bowl of quartz as pink as salmon-eggs;
And deep in the apple-green, a shimmering school
Of trout, like shifting silver dregs.

READERS OF LOAM

Wet loam below a mountain waterfall
Is like a tattered page from out a book,
Rich with high tales of passing mountain folk . . .

Look! in the silt that rims the pool and holds
The milky flood in a black cup of onyx—
Here! in the broken ferns, a crippled elk
Tarried a moment in his flight, to drink,
To nibble at the birch; and on his heels,
Flinging from lustful tongues a foam, flecked red
As any livid toadstool, came coyotes! four! . . .

Here! where the rill meanders a silver yarn
Among the brackens, looping their broken jade,
Ptarmigan stepped like solemn wooden soldiers,
A mother and her palpitating brood.
Spearing a globe of crystal water, each
Soberly rolled it down his gullet, blinked
A crimson lid, and pecked at the dryad's pollen. . . .

And where the chokecherry blossoms drip a fragrance
Upon the air, a grizzly bear came shuffling.
Here, in the patch of adder's-tongue, he clawed
The earth for succulence; there he sniffed,
And tunneled to a nest of meadow-mice;
Yonder he sprawled upon the bank, to drink,
To paw the honey-bees, to contemplate
The blue-finned grayling gliding in the pool. . . .

Oh, there will come a day, when some sharp eye
Will fall upon this range, and mark this pool,
When some keen reader of the great green Book
Will come on footprints in the Loam and say:

"Out of a land of alkali and sage-brush,
Fevered of lip, he staggered to these hills,
Pursued by desert wolves who had no spine
To snarl their jaws at him, save in a pack.
And here upon the thick wet mountain-moss
He flung himself to rest among the brookmints
Cool with the dew, to dream a little, to drink
The cold green wine of earth; and in the evening
He stood upon his legs again, refreshed.

"There, in the balsam grove, he built a flame
And cedar shelter against the frost of night.
And yonder, where the jasper cliff juts out
Over a sea of combering valley pines,
Like any wolf that freezes on a butte
And spills the hunger of his solitude
Into the desert coulees, he flung his call,
And waited for a dusky mate to answer. . . .

"Here, with the cunning of a cougar, he made
A wide detour, scenting a tainted air,
The strychnine in the carcass of a deer;
And there, where the junipers are trampled down
And beaded with blood, he put a careless foot
Upon a trap and felt the crunch of bone
Between sharp teeth unyielding as a badger's;

185

Yonder, with ugly laughter on his lips,
He set his naked hands upon the trap,
And forced its jaws to gap with bloody mirth;
And winning free, he went his way again. . . .

"Here! on this lookout ridge at timber-line,
With sun cascading over him, he sprawled
Deep in the wintergreens, and sank his pain
In mellow dreams—he gave himself to beauty:
The alpine-lily whose brimming cup he tipped
Until he spilled its wine upon the grass;
The clouds that billowed up the mountainside
And washed their silver foam about his knees;
The pinewood's smoke that put a pencil-mark
Upon the horizon, spiralled up the blue,
And scrawled its lazy pungent syllables
Across the sunset—these delighted him. . . .

"And here, beneath the great-armed Douglas fir,
Where stars slip by on quiet feet, and winds
Shake out a slender music from the boughs,
He mingled his body with the dust again. . . .

"Step softly here! among these pulsing flowers
Rooted upon his clay. Put down no foot
Upon their petals; bruise no crimson stem.
These bloodroot blossoms are alive with him."

PART IX

COUNCIL-FIRES

THE WINDS OF FIFTY WINTERS *

The Weasel-Eye, the hawk-nosed one,
With the long white beard and soft white hands,
Arose before the Pillagers and Ottertails
Who squatted by the council-fire.
Fixing on his nose the little windows,
And putting on his face a pretty smile,
The Weasel-Eye "made talk, big talk":

THE WEASEL-EYE TALKS:

"My brothers, good red brothers,
Brothers each and all,
By me, his honest trusted agent
Whose heart is good to the Indian,
The Great White Chief sends greetings
To his good red children—
Ah! and many pretty presents!"

Ho!
Hi-yáh! Hi-yáh!
How! How! How!
Wuh!

"Gaze ye!—Flashing silver-glass
And tinkling copper bells!
And powder kegs and beads,
And tall black shining hats!

---

* For supplementary notes on "The Winds of Fifty Winters" and
other poems in Part IX, see *Appendix,* page 349.

Ye shall walk arrayed
Like yon gorgeous blazing sun
If ye but heed my counsel."

Ho! Ho! Ho!

"Go ye North!
Forsake these rolling hills,
This vast, this too-vast country.
Forsake these wolf-infested forests,
That Pale-Face tillers of the soil
May lay their Iron-Roads
And scratch the ground for harvests.
Go ye North! to the barren lands,
To the land of the marked-out ground.
And though there be no moose
Within its flame-swept timber,
Nor whitefish in its waters,
Nor patches of wild berries,
Nor fields of nodding rice,
Yet will ye be content
For I shall pay ye well:
To every warrior, guns—
Six beavers' worth;
To every headman, blankets—
Red as yonder sky;
To every chieftain, ponies—
Six, more or less.
And there, in the marked-out North,
Your tribe may eat and dance
Forever and forever.

"Gaze upon me, O my brothers,
My good red brothers,
And heed ye well my counsel!
The winds of fifty winters
Have blown about my head,
And, lo! my hair is white with snow!
The winds of fifty winters
Have blown about my head,
And, lo! much wisdom lodged therein!
And from the winds of fifty winters,
Their wisdom, storms, and snows,
Lo! I counsel ye:
Sign ye this treaty!
Take ye the presents!
Go ye to the North!"

In the council-grove long silence fell,
But for a little laughing wind
That wandered in the pines.
Then, sinuous and supple as the wildcat,
Áh-nah-mah-keé, the "Thunderbolt," strode forward.
He stood a moment silent—
Straight as the Norway pine
That rears its head above the timber;
And in his eyes the many little lightnings flashed,
But on the corner of his mouth a sunbeam played:

THUNDERBOLT TALKS:

"O my brothers, my red brothers,
Brothers each and all,

The Weasel-Eye has spoken.
He has opened up his honey mouth;
And from the heart that is so good
He has poured his sounding words.
His heap-much pretty talk
Is like the tinkling stream
Of babbling sweet-water that gurgles
Down from the mountain springs;
But like the sweet-water of the brook,
That stops its pretty running
In the swamp and stands one sleep
In the deep and quiet pools,
The pretty words turn bitter-sour.

"Gaze upon me, O my brothers,
My good red brothers!
The winds of fifty winters
Have blown about my head,
And, lo! my hair is white with snow!
The winds of fifty winters
Have blown about my head,
And, lo! much wisdom lodged therein!
The winds of fifty winters
Have blown about my head—
But, lo! They have not blown away my brains!

"I am done!"

> *Ho!*
> *Hi! Hi!*
> *How! How! How!*

MEDALS AND HOLES

Boo-zhóo nee-chée! Me—Yellow-Otter,
I'm going mak'-um big-talk, 'Spector Jone'.

Look-see!—on chest I'm got-um golden medal;
Got-um woman on medal. Ho!—good medal!

Me—I'm go to Washin'ton long tam' ago;
Me—I'm tell-um Kéetch-ie Ó-gi-má, dose Big W'ite Chief:
"Eenzhuns no lak-um Eenzhun rese'vation;
No good! She's too much jack-pine, sand, and swamp."
Big-chief, him say: "Ó-zah-wah-kíg, you be good boy!
Go back to rese'vation. You tell-um tribe
If Eenzhun stay on rese'vation, Washin'ton gov'ment
Give-um all de Eenzhuns plenty payments, every year;
Give-um plenty good hats and suits o' clothes.
My heart is good to you; you damned good Eenzhun.
Me—I'm stick-um dis golden medal on your chest."
Ho! I'm walk-um home. I got-um medal—look-see!

But—me—no got-um plenty good hats and clothes;
No got-um every year; only every two year.
Clothes no good! Look-see! Got-um clothes on now—
No good! Got-um holes in legs—plenty-big holes
Wit' not much clot' around; and too much buttons off.
Gov'ment clothes she's coming every two year—
Long tam' between, too much—wit' too much holes.

Before de w'ite man come across Big-Water,
In olden tam', de Eenzhun got-um plenty clothes;

193

He mak'-um plenty suits wit' skins—no holes.
Even Shing-óos, dose weasel, and dose snowshoe rabbit,
Dey got-um better luck—two suits every year—
Summer, brown-yellow suit; winter, w'ite suit—
No got-um holes.
Wau-góosh and Nee-gíg, dose fox and otter,
Shang-wáy-she, dose mink, Ah-méek, dose beaver,
Dey get-um plenty clothes, each year two suits—
Summer, t'in clothes; winter, t'ick fur clothes—
No got-um holes.
Wásh-kish, dose big buck deer, and moose,
Each year dey t'row away deir horns;
In summer dey get-um nice new hat—
No got-um holes.
Me—I'm big-smart man, smarter dan weasel,
Smarter dan moose and fox and beaver;
Me—I'm also smart Eenzhun;
I got-um golden medal on chest from Big-Knife Chief;
But me—I'm only got-um one suit clothes
In two year—no-good clothes, no-good hats!
'Spector Jone', you tell-um our Big-Knife Preshident so:
"Yellow-Otter no got-um plenty good clothes;
No got-um silk-black hat, no stove-pipes hat;
Him got-um plenty-much holes in Washin'ton pants."
Tell-um holes in pants now big, plenty-big—
Bigger dan golden medal on chest!

So much—dat's enough.

How! How!
Kay-gét! Kay-gét!
Ho! Ho! Ho!

Boo-zhóo, Inspector Taylo',
Me—I talk-um for all dose Eenzhuns
She's sitting by dose pine-trees.
Agent-man from Kéetch-ie Ó-gi-má,
Our Big W'ite Chief on Washin'ton,
De heart of all de 'Cheebway
In my tribe are good to you;
My people want your heart
Be good to all de Eenzhuns.

In E'ghteen E'ghty-nine,
In Summer-of-de-Many-Rains,
Comes Kéetch-ie Móh-ka-món,
De Big-Knife, w'ite man, Major Rice,
An' black-robed priest, for mak'-um treaty.
Dey mak'-um talk in council, so:
" 'Cheebway, 'Cheebway, mak'-um treaty;
Walk on far-away reservation an' live;
You go new reservation, you get-um plenty t'ing
From Kéetch-ie Ó-gi-má,
De w'ite man's Preshident:
You get-um plenty grub an' money;
Plenty t'ing for belly an' for back."

Den Big-Knife stick-um one hand
On Big-Black-Book an' treaty-paper,
An' raise-um oder hand to Kéetch-ie Má-ni-dó,
De w'ite man's Big Spirit, an' say:
" 'Cheebway, all dose t'ing on treaty sure will be!" . . .

195

Ho! Eenzhun scratch-um paper;
Stick-um t'umb on treaty;
An' walk-um on new reservation.

W'at's come treaty now! Ugh?

No got-um plenty money-payment!
No got-um plenty grub!
'Cheebway got-um small flat belly;
No got-um w'ite man's big fat belly.

Comes soon Bee-bóan, de Winter-Maker,
Blowing on de river wit' hees icy breat',
An' making dem stand still
Wit' sleep beneat' de snow.
An' Nort' Wind whistle crazy-wild
T'rough crying spruce an' cedar;
Den Múk-wa, ol' fat bear, he sleep
An' sheever in hees hole in de groun';
An' Pée-nay, hungry pa'tridge,
Bury in de balsam snow-drif'.

Now walk on Eenzhun wéeg-i-wam, in winter!
'Cheebway sit dere hungry—
In winter no can get-um grub lak moose
Who paw big hole in snow for plenty moss.
No got-um plenty money;
No got-um plenty w'ite man's grub.
Eenzhun squaw, she got-um sick—
Bad osh-kée-shee-gwá-pee-náy—
She got-um Sick-on-eye—trachom'—

She no can see—no can do.
Squáw-sich, little gal,
She got-um measles-sick,
De Spotted-Sickness on de face.
Little boy, he got-um heap-sick—
Bad óh-pun-náh-pee-náy—
Bad Sickness-on-de-lung;
Ugh! He spit all-tam'!—wit' blood!
Got-um sick on chest an' hot on cheek—
Got-um eye she blaze lak wildcat! . . .
W'y should be dose t'ing?
Ugh! Go w'ite man's town:
He's got-um plenty grub;
Hees belly laugh wit' grub!
He's no got-um squaw
She's got-um Sick-on-eye;
He's no got-um leetle boy
She's got-um Sickness-on-de-lung!

W'y should be diff'rence, ha-aaah?
Mebbe w'ite man's God he want-um diff'rence! Ugh!
Mebbe Kéetch-ie Má-ni-dó no lak-um Eenzhun chil'en! Hah!
Mebbe Kéetch-ie Má-ni-dó forget-um Eenzhun chil'en! Ugh!
Mebbe so! Mebbe so! . . .

Mebbe *no!*
Look-um straight!
Talk-um straight!
Ai-yee! Kéetch-ie Má-ni-dó
He *no* forget-um 'Cheebway Eenzhun!
Kéetch-ie Má-ni-dó he lak-um Eenzhun chil'en

Just so much he lak-um Big-Knife chil'en!
Eenzhun chil'en, good chil'en!

Ho! Ho!
How! How!

Inspector Taylo',
In council of olden tam',
In E'ghteen E'ghty-nine,
W'en Major Rice stick-um hand on Big-Black-Book,
An' raise-um oder hand to sky an' say:
" 'Cheebway! all dose t'ing on treaty-paper sure will be!"

Mebbe . . . mebbe . . .
Mebbe . . . w'en he was say dose t'ing . . .
Mebbe he was only fool for fun! Hah?
Ho! Big-Knife only fool for fun! Ho!

Mebbe so! . . . Mebbe so! . . .

Mebbe hees tongue talk-um
Little bit crooked! Ho?
Mebbe so! . . . Mebbe so! . . .

Mebbe he got-um forks in tongue,
Wit' little poison-gland!
Lak snake! Hah?

Mebbe so! . . . Mebbe so! . . .

Eenzhun t'ink . . . Eenzhun t'ink:
He lie!

198

Look on me! . . .
Look on me! . . .
Look on me! . . .

Talk-um straight, Inspector Taylo',
Talk-um straight *today!*
No got-um double-snake-tongue! . . .

So much—dat's enough!
I have said it!

    Ho!
    How! How!
    Ho! Ho! Ho!

Boo-zhóo! Boo-zhóo!
Me, Áh-deek-kóons, I mak'-um big talk.
Me, ol' man; I'm got-um sick on knee
In rainy wedder w'en I'm walk. Ugh!
Me, lak moose w'at's ol',
I'm drop-um plenty toot'!
Yet I am big man! Ho!
An' I am talk-um plenty big! Ho!

  Hi-yee! Blow lak moose, ol' man!
  Ho! Ho!

  Hi-yi! Little-Caribou him talk
  Lak Ó-mah-kah-kée, dose Bullfrog:
  Big mout', big belly,
  No can fight!

Ugh! Close mout', young crazy buck!
You stop-um council-talk,
You go 'way council!
Sit wit' squaw!
You lak little Poh-tóong,
Lak pollywog tad-pole:
No can jump-um
Over little piece mud;
Can only shake-um tail
Lak crazy fool! . . .

Kéetch-ie Ó-gi-má, Big Preshiden',
He got-um plenty t'oughts in head;

Me, Caribou, I'm got-um plenty-good t'oughts,
Got-um plenty-good t'oughts in head.
Yet Eenzhun-Agent all-tam' saying:
"Áh-deek-kóons, he crazy ol' fool!"
Ugh! *He* crazy ol' fool!

Kéetch-ie Ó-gi-má long tam' ago
Was say in Pine Point Treaty:
"All de 'Cheebway should be farmer;
All will get from Washin'ton gov'ment
Good allotment farm land,
One hondred-sixty acre each." Ho!
Ho! Eenzhun scratch-um treaty.
Stick-um t'umb on treaty.

W'at's come treaty? Hah?
Eenzhun got-um hondred-sixty acre,
But got-um too much little pieces—
Pieces scattered over lake
Lak leaves she's blow by wind.
In tam'rack swamp by Moose Tail Bay
He got-um forty acre piece.
Ten mile away, on Lake of Cut-foot Sioux,
In mush-káig an' in swampland,
He got-um forty acre more.
On Bowstring Lake, she's t'orty mile away,
In sand and pickerel weed,
He got-um forty acre more.
Hondred mile away, on Lac La Croix,
W'ere lumberman is mak' big dam
For drive-um log—an' back-um up water

All over Eenzhun allotment land—
He got-um forty acre more—all under lake!
How can Eenzhun be good farmer! Ugh?
He's got-um land all over lake!
He's got-um land all under lake!
For Eenzhun be good farmer
Eenzhun should be good for walking under water!
Should be plow hees land wit' clam-drag!
Should be gadder potato crops wit' fish-net!
For Eenzhun be good farmer
Eenzhun should be fish!
Ugh!

I have said it!

> *Ho! Ho! Ho!*
> *Hi! Hi! Plenty-big talk!*
> *How!*

FIRE-BENDER TALKS

Fire-Bender wants talk-um now
On Treaty of E'ghteen E'ghty-nine.

Major Rice, de gov'ment man,
Him scratch on treaty, so:
"When Eenzhun give-um up hees land,
Wherever Eenzhun go and live,
Den Washin'ton mak'-it good for him
So he can hunt all-tam' lak in olden tam'."

Comes now Minnesota game-warden,
Police of deer and moose and fishing;
He got-um silver star on chest,
He got-um plenty big mout'.
He tak'-um on jail two Eenzhun boy
She's kill wan deer, and den he say:
" 'Cheebway, you no can hunt-um moose
Or deer outside de hunting season;
You kill dose wásh-kish, dose w'ite-tail deer,
In summer, you pay-um fifty irons;
Dat's 'gainst the Big-Knife's law!
In Treaty E'ghteen E'ghty-nine
De 'Cheebway scratch-um 'way deir hunting rights."

'Spector Taylo', you be smart man—
You t'ink dat Eenzhun she's damn fool?
You t'ink she's scratch-um 'way hees grub?
You t'ink she's give-um 'way hees right for live?

Ugh! 'Cheebway no can live except
Wan way: on grub she's in de water
And animal she's on land.
Kéetch-ie Má-ni-dó, Big-Spirit,
Mak'-it so de w'ite man get-um grub
By scratching ground wit' crazy-stick;
By making mud laugh up wit' plenty corn;
By digging hole in granite rock
And taking plenty copper-iron
Out of de guts of ground.
Same God He's mak'-um grub
For all dose Big-Knife w'ite man
He's mak'-um grub for Eenzhuns;
He's mak'-um for Eenzhun all dose t'ing
She's jump in water and on de land:
He's mak'-um pickerel and w'itefish,
O-gáh, dose pike, and wée-bee-zhéen,
Dose skipjacks and silver tulibees;
He's mak'-um sturgeon and másh-ke-nón-zhay,
And all dose fish she's walking in de lake.
He's mak'-um deer and elk, she's running
Wild in de timber and big mush-káig;
He's mak'-um caribou and moose,
She's feed in de lily in de river.
Ho! same big má-ni-dó
He's mak'-um grub for Big-Knife chil'en
Mak'-um grub for Eenzhun chil'en.

'Spector Taylo', you ask-um warden
If she's forget-um dose olden treaty;
You ask-um if w'ite man mak'-um newer treaty,

Wit' *God*—if Big-Spirit scratch on paper so:
"Only de w'ite man, beginning now,
Belongs him de sea, de land, de sky,
And all dose fish and animal and bird
She's walk in de water, de ground, de air."
Mebbe—mebbe dose Big-Knife warden
She's got-um treaty-paper lak dat! Ho!
Me—I lak see—me—dose paper
For treaty w'ite man mak' wit' God.
Me—I lak see—me—dose paper!

So much I say—no more.

Ho! Ho!
Kay-gét!

WHIRLING-RAPIDS TALKS

Boo-zhóo, Inspector Taylor,
I, Wáh-wee-yáh-tun-ung, Chief Whirling-Rapids,
Make this talk, "big talk," for all my people.

In eighteen eighty-nine
The Big-Knife soldier
Called council with the Ojibways on Pine Point,
And there he made this big and pretty talk:
"K'tchée-gah-mee Indians, men of the land of the Big-Water,
Today we will make a good treaty;
Go to the marked-out reservation;
Here will come no white men;
Here will ye hunt and dance in peace,
Free from all the Big-Knives."

Ho! Good talk! Pretty talk!

> *Ho!*
> *Ugh!*
> *Ho! Ho!*

Ugh! Talk now of the Treaty of Pine Point!
Comes too much white man on the reservation!
My people know the story.
It is marked on the slashed pine,
And the burned timbers,
And the scratched earth.
Came the trappers for our beaver;
Came the crazy iron-roads,

And the crazy fire-wagons
Blowing devil's-noise—
Ugh!
Came the loggers with their axes,
With their flashing iron axes;
And our mighty forests trembled
From the cursings—from the clashings
Of the irons everywhere—
Ugh!
Came the rat-eyed little traders
With their shining silver clocks,
Their eésh-kwo-dáy-wah-bóo,
Their plenty fire-water,
Their plenty devil's-spit—
Ugh!
Came many, many Big-Knives,
Pretty on the outside,
Rotten in the heart;
From the many, many towns
Came many waves of white men—
Big wave, big wave,
Wave, wave, wave.
And my people wither like the oak-leaves;
And hunger stalks about my village;
And sickness spots my little children;
And often in the Moon-of-Freezing
The chantings for the dead are as many
As the wailings of the starving coyotes
Ai-yeee! Pity us!
Ai-yeee! Pity us!

Little wave, little wave,
Big wave, big wave,
Wave, wave, wave—
So comes the white man in the North,
Like the waters of the ocean.
On the waters of that sea walks the Indian
In his frail and battered chée-mon,
In his tossing birch canoe,
And he paddles from the dawn to the twilight.
Comes the little rippling water on the bow,
Little white fingers rippling on the birch-bark,
Rippling white fingers blowing in the wind.
Comes little wave of white men,
Little wave, little wave,
Many pretty waves.
Comes bigger wave of white men,
Bigger wave of white men,
Big waves, big waves,
Tumbling into the silver shore,
Rumbling as they come;
Foaming, roaring, leaping billows,
Bending like the weeping willows,
Rolling up and tumbling over,
Rolling,
Rolling,
Rolling up and rolling under,
Growling with a mighty thunder—
Higher, higher, leaping higher—
Flashing tongues across the sky,
Fire in the crackling clouds, fire!—
Wave, wave, wave,

Rolling up and tumbling over,
Shattering silver spray
On the Indian in the chée-mon,
Battering iron fists upon his birch-bark—
Crazy laughing crazy-waters,
Crazy hands and crazy arms
Splashing wildly in the wind,
Crashing madly on the tossing birch-bark,
Smashing wildly at the wailing 'Cheebway . . .

And the Indian walking on the waters
Flings his chantings to the Spirits in the sky:

> *"Hah-eee-ooooo! Kéetch-ie Má-ni-dó,*
> *I sing the chant of death!*
> *O pity me!*
> *And stop the crazy-waters,*
> *Ai-yee! the rolling waves of white men. . . .*
> *O pity me!*
> *Hah-eee-ooooo! Kéetch-ie Má-ni-dó!*
> *I am asking with a good heart. . . .*

"Ai-yee! The Spirit cannot hear me;
Nothing does he hear
But the clashing iron axes,
The rumblings of the waters,
And the cursings in the timber on the shore. . . .

"Ai-yee! He hurls his balls of fire,
Fiercely crashing in the timber—
In the timber
There is Death!

"O pity me!

"Ai-yee! He lashes at his clouds,
At his frightened shivering clouds,
With his whips
Of cracking wind!

"O pity me!

"Ai-yee! He lunges with his spear,
With his double-lightning spear,
At the trembling
Little chée-mon!

"O pity me! . . .
O pity me! . . ."

   .   .   .   .

Look! He plunges at the wailing 'Cheebway—
Look!—With crazy hands of crazy-waters! . . .
Lo! and Death walks with the Indian
On the bottom of the lake,
Beneath the crazy-waters,
Crashing up and rolling over . . .
Crashing up . . . and rolling over . . .
Rolling . . . rolling . . .
Rolling over . . . over . . .

   .   .   .   .

Now the dripping sun is laughing in the rainbow-sky,
On the quivering silver birches on the land;
And the laughing little waters with their little white feet,
Run pattering on the shifting yellow sand.

But the Devil-Spirit, Múch-ie Má-ni-dó,
Is walking on the bottom of the lake,
In the drifting tangled weeds,
In the water shimmering green
Where the fishes flash
And shiver in the sun.
He is shaking his big belly,
He is winking his red eye
At the Big-Knife who stands chuckling
Where the waters wash the shore,
At the buzzard-taloned white man
Who stands looking at the bottom of the waters.

Ugh! Crazy Big-Knife! . . .

Ugh! Crazy Devil! . . .

Ai-ee! Drifting body
That lies tangled in the weeds!

I have said it!

> *Ho!*
> *How! How! How!*
> *Ho!*

PART X

TINDER AND FLINT

COVENANT WITH EARTH

So! It is darkly written: I must go,
Go shadowed by sorrow as my father went,
Hurled in his highest moment earthward, spent,
Like a shattered falling arrow from a bow.

Oh, let it stand! No syllable of grief
Shall tremble on my lips, no teary brine
Dribble upon an open wound of mine.

Once having looked upon an autumn leaf,
Palsied and scourged, a soaring eagle slain,
And rose-leaves pelted down to dust by rain—
I came to understand the blind earth's way,
Her calm indifference to shattered clay,
Her will to tramp on flesh with the iron cleat
Of anguish, failure, bitterness, defeat.
As an intimate of earth I came to know
That this gaunt wretched moment long ago
Was written in my covenant with the soil;
That all who hold a lien on life contract
With the elemental earth to hold the pact
Subject to all its varied terms, its sweet,
Its bitter, its endless trouble and its toil.
Too well I came to know that a groan, a curse,
Shall never change the inexorable fact
That flesh must break, for better or for worse.

Hear me, O stern Inscrutable-One! Rough-hew
To a barbed and tortuous point whatever lance

Of pain you will, or of harrowing circumstance,
And plunge it through my ribs from out the blue.
The thrust shall find me dry-eyed, resolute,
Dropping no moan—whatever blood shall spill;
As imperturbable as any brute,
As taciturn as stone upon a hill.

REQUIEM FOR A MODERN CROESUS

To him the moon was a silver dollar, spun
Into the sky by some mysterious hand; the sun
Was a gleaming golden coin—
His to purloin;
The freshly minted stars were dimes of delight
Flung out upon the counter of the night.

In yonder room he lies,
With pennies on his eyes.

WORDS

He never flinched, and never a muscle stirred;
Speechless he stood beneath the stinging whips
She laid upon him in each syllable
    That crackled from her lips.

Yet in his heart a river of anger rolled,
And swept his words into a groaning jam,
As when a torrent chokes a rushing stream
    With logs across a dam.

But when she flung at him the dynamite
Of epithet and insinuating doubt,
With a mighty moan the pent-up tide gave way,
    And the jam of words went out:

Words cut by a madman's ax; words brittle with ice;
Words pointed, barbed with sleet and torn of branch;
Words that cascaded, ricocheted, and split,
    Fell in an avalanche.

Down with the flood of wrath they pitched and plunged,
Until at last there came the utter peace
That settles on a stream when logs go out,
    And flood-tides find release.

GOD IS AT THE ANVIL

God is at the anvil, beating out the sun;
    Where the molten metal spills,
    At His forge among the hills
He has hammered out the glory of a day that is done.

God is at the anvil, welding golden bars;
    In the scarlet-streaming flame
    He is fashioning a frame
For the shimmering silver beauty of the evening stars.

DUST

This much I know:
Under the bludgeonings of snow
And sleet and sharp adversity,
From high estate
The seemingly immortal tree
Shall soon or late
Go down to dust;
When a wild wet gust
Tumbles the gaunt debris
Down from the gashed plateau
And out upon the plain,
The dust shall go
Down with the rain;
Rivers are slow,
Rivers are fast,
But rivers and rains run down to the sea,
All rains go down to the sea at last.

Oh, shake the red bough,
And cover me now,
Cover me now with dreams,
With a blast
Of falling leaves, with the filtered gleams
Of the moon;
Shake the dead bough
And cover me now,
For soon
Rivers and rains shall go with me
Down to the vast infinity.

BLACK OMEN

Out of the slanting dusk it came—
The thought too sinister for words;
With wings that flapped against the moon
More darkly swift than any bird's.

As a bat all night above a pond
Shadows the mirrored firmament,
It flecked my tranquil pool of dreams;
And like a bat at dawn it went.

The little cabin seems to wear
Such a panic-stricken air—
Clinging perilously high
Silhouetted on the sky.

There is such a tragic fear
In the furtive eyes that peer
Down upon the ocean's jaw,
Red and ravenous of maw.

Such a terror in her soul
When the casual pebbles roll—
Oh, the frantic nervous gripping,
Fearful that her hands are slipping.

Such a never-ending dread
Of the forest overhead—
Wondering when the inching spruce
Will crowd her aching fingers loose.

LITTLE ENOUGH THERE IS OF WORTH

Little enough there is of worth
On this green ball of earth:
Wind in a hemlock-tree, to shake
A cool wet music from the brake;
Flame in an earthen bowl
To warm a frozen soul
And cheer a heart grown chill
With solitude and ill;
And water in a rill,
Rimmed round with moss that drips
Upon the rock, until it fashions
A goblet for hot lips,
A cup for futile passions.

And when the high heart is broken,
The last word spoken,
And tears are many as the dew—
The fragmentary dreams
Of beauty that the world discloses
In every woodland, these are sweet,
My bread, my wine, my meat:
October smoke that hovers on the streams
And spirals up the blue;
Clambering mountain-roses,
By tender-fingered rain unfurled;
And honey-laden bees
That nuzzle the buds of shy anemones,
And dust a golden pollen on the world.

But rarer far than these—
Than any flower-cup or pool
From which to drink one's fill
Of loveliness, a potion beaded, cool,
To fortify the will—
I hold the sanguine hue
Of dawn, when courage springs anew
And the heart is high
As the banners of the day go up the sky;
The wine of the setting sun that holds
A promise of a glad tomorrow;
The pool of moonlight that enfolds
The sable hills and hollows—
As the quivering silver cry
Of a lost lone loon
Answers the drowsy swallow's,
And faintly the echoes die—
The pool of mountain moon
In which to fling oneself and make an
end of sorrow.

MARCHING PINES

Up the drifted foothills,
　Like phantoms in a row,
The ragged lines of somber pines
　Filed across the snow.

Down the gloomy coulees
　The burdened troopers went,
Snowy packs upon their backs,
　Bowed of head and bent.

Up the cloudy mountains,
　A mournful singing band,
Marching aimless to some nameless,
　Undiscovered land.

YELLOW MOON

O yellow moon,
Drifting across the night
As a rakish pirate brig,
Tattered of rig
And ghostly white,
Goes floating down the black lagoon
Of a dead sea—
O pirate moon,
Out of your hatch and hold
Pour down your buccaneering beams,
Your pirates, swaggering and bold,
And bid them capture me;
O ghostly moon,
Carry me out to the farthest sweep
Of the slow tides of sleep;
Abandon me upon the gold
Of some enchanted strand,
Where the blue-flame comber gleams
And breaks upon the sand;
Oh, sail with me to a far land
Of unremembered dreams.

OAK

An implacable granite-breasted god
    Scourges me low,
Lays on my flesh a merciless rod—
    Even so.

Drawing his lightning saber of grief
    From the scabbard of blue,
He sinks it in me beyond belief—
    Oh, true! true!

What though distress like a shower of stone
    Rains from the sky,
Who shall go down to the earth with a moan?
    Not I!

Long have I known that a cry is spent breath;
    That weeping will not
Vary the shuttles of life and death
    By even a jot.

Try me, grim god, with your pitiless sword;
    I shall not quail,
But stand toe to toe with my savage lord—
    An oak in a gale.

TRAILING ARBUTUS

I found a wild arbutus in the dell,
The first-born blossom from the womb of spring;
The bud, unfurling, held me in a spell
With its hesitant awakening.

Fragrant its petals, pink and undefiled
As the palm of one new-born, or its finger-tips;
Delicate as the song of a little child,
And sweet as the breath between its lips.

Something in shy arbutus wet with dew
Lays hold of me, something I do not know—
Unless—among these blossoms once I knew
A little boy, oh, long ago.

FIR OF THE YULE

Out of tempestuous wilderness
You came, O fir—a swampland drear
With tumult of snow and the wind's stress,
Where the wolf's wail cuts a livid scar
Through blanching night to the farthest star;
Out of a solitude where, year
On patient year, above the feud
Of clashing elements that swirled
About you in a dismal world,
You bore yourself with fortitude,
Spartan, unbowed of head, serene.

Out of the waste where the wind brawls,
Into these four drab city walls
You came, O buoyant fir, to cheer
With your supple, clean, untroubled green,
Children of sorrow lingering here.

Though all the stormy world shall knock
Insistent knuckles on our door
And fumble snarling at the lock,
Yield us, O stoic visitor,
A measure of your unconcern;
Yield us, who linger at your side
Throughout this gentle Christmastide,
Your spirit, calm and taciturn,
A precious moment of release,
The benediction of your peace.

WINTER OAK

The horizon cleaved the world in halves: the sky
    A pure cerulean blue;
The prairie snow unwrinkled as a sheet,
    Of spotless ivory hue.

Unmarred the azure, immaculate the plain,
    But for an ancient oak
Wrapped in a cloud of frozen yellow leaves
    That clung like a golden cloak.

Oh, for a wind to sully the white, a cloud
    To smudge the celestial girth!—
Too much there was of heaven in the world,
    And not enough of earth.

LEAVE ME TO MY OWN

Oh, leave me to my own;
Unglorified, unknown,
One of a nameless band
Of gypsy cloud and silent butte and fir.
Oh, let me stand
Against the whipping wind, in the lavender
Of dusk, like a mighty limber-pine
At timber-line—
Unyielding, stiff,
Unbent of head
Among the ageless dead—
One with the mountain's cliff
And the imperturbable stone.

And when the winter gales intone
Among my boughs a dread
And melancholy sweep
Of song, and some mysterious hand
Brushes my heart
In a mournful melody, weep
No tear for me, nor moan—
Pray, stand apart
From me, and leave me to my own;
For in the high blue valleys of this land,
When the afterglow
Lingers among the glaciers, I shall know
Again the calm
Of dusk, the dewy balm

Of sleep, release
From pain—and utter peace.

Oh, leave me to the wild companionship
Of firs that toss
In the windy night and drip
Their wild wet rains upon the moss;
To the columbine
That strives to slip
Shyly among my roots and tip
Its sparkling wine
Upon my grassy shrine;
To the brotherhood
Of bending skies bestrown
With stars above the soundless solitude—
Of waterfalls that fling upon the night
A stony broken music from their height—
Oh, leave me to my own.

SWAMP-OWL

A brooding pond in the hush of dusk,
   As black as the pool of night;
Rimmed round with spires of somber spruce—
   Gaunt ghosts in the phantom light.

A beating of heavy wings in the dark;
   A rush from the dismal glen;
A sudden swoop, and the leaden wings
   Went beating back again.

In the utter gloom of that sunken land,
   Never a creature stirred,
As night beat into the sullen swamp
   With the wings of that ghostly bird.

INDIAN SUMMER

When I went down the butte to drink at dawn,
   I saw a frozen lily by the spring,
A ragged stream-line rank of whistling swan,
   And the swift flash of a willet's wing.

And now comes a hint of winter in the air:
   Among the pensive valleys drifts a haze
Of dusty blue, and the quaking-asp lies bare
   To the chill breath of hoary days.

Farewell, my mountain-ash and goldenrod,
   For summer swoons in autumn's arms, and dies,
As the languid rivers drowse and the asters nod
   Beneath the gray wind's lullabies.

Farewell, my fleet-foot antelope and doe;
   Farewell, my wild companions of the hills—
Soon in your winter-slumber you will go
   To a far land of singing rills.

Soon by the fire I'll sit with quiet dreams;
   .In the sinuous smoke, silver against the blue,
That floats above the dusky vales and streams,
   My eyes will see the ghosts of you.

I'll ride my night-patrols upon the peak—
   And the big wind among the firs, the lone
Wandering wolf, and the waterfall will speak
   Of you in a language of their own.

We'll miss you, blue-eyed grass and laughing brook;
  In the spring on some high mesa we'll confer,
And with shining eyes we'll trace your form, and look
  For you when your snowy blankets stir.

Rest well, my comrades; know that while you sleep,
  With eager hearts we'll listen for your song,
And through the night a patient watch we'll keep
  For you—don't stay away too long.

TIMBER-LINE CEDAR

Ho! patriarchal cedar, torn
By bitter winds, and weather-worn,
How came your countenance so stark,
Disconsolate, and dark.

In hermit-souls I've never seen
So gnarled and dolorous a mien—
Such a mournful misanthrope
Bereft of faith and hope.

Can it be your figure spare
Is due to slender mountain-fare?
Your limbs awry with rheumatic pains
From chilling autumn rains?

How came the choler-twisted mouth?—
Wrangling with the wind and drouth?
And how the beaten head and branch?—
Ruthless avalanche?

What! Within your scanty shade,
Sharing life with you, a blade!—
Sheltered by a withered root,
A lupine at your foot!

Deceiver! Holding in the bower
Of your breast a fragile flower—
When every gesture seems to hint
A heart of solid flint—

I know you now for what you are:
A roguish beau, grown angular
And gruff, but still at heart quite gentle,
And highly sentimental.

BITTERN

I saw against the sunset's tangerine
  An umber bittern fly,
Flapping his heavy wings in the evergreen,
  Croaking his hollow cry.

He stretched his eager neck from left to right,
  Craning to find a nook
Where he might stilt himself through solemn night
  In a quiet bend of brook.

At dusk I saw him on a sunken log,
  Bronze in the sunset's blood,
Slumbering, undisturbed by the trilling frog,
  And the beaver-tail's dull thud.

THE GREAT DIVIDE

When I drift out on the Silver Sea,
O may it be
A blue night
With a white moon
And a sprinkling of stars in the cedar-tree;
And the silence of God,
And the low call
Of a lone bird. . . .

A congress of bullfrogs jowl-deep in the slime,
To the droll moon was croaking its notions of rime.
And puffy with pride each wight in the throng
Expounded with vigor the charm of his song:

"Gr-rump! Gr-rump!" bellowed Greenback, "I sing of the
mud; oh, the beautiful, beautiful mud!"
And he flopped his big belly—ker-plunk!—in the clay
with a heave and a terrible thud.

"Quite r-r-right! Quite r-r-right!" rejoined the philosophic
band,
"Sing of the true, the real, of the common thing at hand."

"Ker-r-r-chug!" piped Yellow-Vest, "I sing of the slimy
pond;
Eternal Beauty is there, and not in the moons beyond."

"Yer-r r-right!" quoth Plunk, "but don't be silly;
Praise not the slime, but its flowering, the lily."

"Get along-ng-ng! though flowers are sweet," scoffed
Blink, "we'll not concede a jot!
Vermin nest in the hearts of flowers; all lilies are touched
with rot!"

"Jug-o'-r-r-rum!" croaked Puff, "why sing of the stars, so
cold, remote, and high!
I pray to a closer, warmer light; I sing of the firefly!"

And thus deriding the heavenly host, this tribe with vocal
    might
And philosophic grunt held forth through many a summer
    night. . . .

Autumn marched in with its bluster and blow;
And winter rushed down with a whirling of snow.
The swamp-world lay dead and the amphibian choir
Slept songless and lean in the beautiful mire,
Where the muck-rooted lilies and slender reeds
Were a mess of rank rubbish and rotting weeds.
And the will-o'-the-wisp, the substitute star,
The ideal of Life, of "things as they are,"
Curled up his carcass and jerked up his knees—
His lamp flickered out in the first autumn breeze.

And the placid old moon widely yawned, slyly blinked;
And the stars with a chuckle looked pond-ward, and winked.

FOREST FIRE

I

Among the brittle needles of the pine,
A crackling ember, casually flung—
Spitting in the tinder of the soil . . .
Writhing crimson vipers
Redly licking at the leaves
With flickering venomous tongues,
Bellying into the amorous wind,
And sinking red tusks in the flank of the night.

II

Lo! blazing mane and streaming bridle,
Bursting out of the lurid hills,
A stallion,
A livid-crimson stallion,
A lightning-pinioned stallion,
Crashing out of the billowing smoke
On a flaming crimson trail.
A ghastly shriek in the canyon,
An echoing moan in the pines,
A wild red rush of flying feet,
And a hand at the charger's bit.
A flame-shod foot in the stirrup,
A phantom hand on the reins—
And vaulting into the saddle,
A rider in scarlet,
A swaggering rider in scarlet,
The ghost of a red dragoon!

A war-brawling wild cavalier,
With a cackle sardonic and grim,
A bite in his whistling arrows,
And a blight in his scorching breath.
Careering he charges the timber
With clouds of resin-hot lances,
And he shouts a demoniac laughter
When his blood-bleary eyes behold
Scurrying out of the riotous hills
A rabble of shadowy things:
Oh, the clatter of whistling deer,
The patter of feet in the rushes,
The bleat of the panting fawn!—
Flung out of the timber like leaves,
Like burning leaves in the wind
Whirled over the hills and the valleys
And out to the fringes of night.

A bloody-lipped red cavalier!
A blasphemous dread cavalier!
Galloping into the cloud-templed hills
With a ribald song in his mouth,
With a curse for the gray-bearded firs
That complain of his searing breath;
Sundering their boles with a molten fist,
Cleaving their suppliant branches,
With a jeer as they go to a thundering doom
Enshrouded in bellowing flame,
As they wing their gray souls
On the spiralling smoke
Up to the ultimate sky.

Galloping over tumultuous clouds
To tilt at the livid-lipped stars;
Galloping on through the turbulent night
And over the rim of the world.

III

Oh, the toll of the rider in scarlet!
The toll of the red dragoon!
Windrows of charred black bones
Strewn over a pocked and gutted land;
Skeletons—once draped in the green
Of leaf and the silken sheen of moss;
Bare skeletons, bitter of laughter,
Clattering through long white nights—
Gray ghosts in a land of ravaged dead,
Playing the bow of the wind futilely
Over the once resonant fiddle,
Striving again to beguile old melodies,
Bemoaning the old sweet Aprils.
O fiddlers, scratching over the shattered box,
And scraping over the tattered strings,
Pray, conjure me a tune: the low call
Of the last singing bird that is gone.

PART XI

FIGURES IN BRONZE

CHIEF BLOODY-FEATHER, A
COUNCIL-CHIEF

Ringed by platoons of stoic bronze, the chief
Stood up in the council-grove above the rabble—
Headmen and chiefs, hunters, jugglers, braves,
The children of his loins, his children's children—
Above this host the council-speaker loomed:
An ancient maple-tree, a strong sweet tree
That has made wild music from the wind and snow
For ninety winters; a maple-tree whose arms,
Stretching against the rain, the bouncing hail,
Has sheltered multitudes of travellers
And straggling hosts of elders, wayworn, broken
And weary with the day—for ninety summers.

A maple that has yielded up its life
Season on sugar-season—oh, what can be
More darkly lovely than an ancient maple:
Swollen and scarred of trunk, and varicose
From gashes in the bark, from too many wounds
Of too many spiles that let out too much sap;
From too much giving, giving for ninety years,
For ninety Moons-of-Maple-Sugar-Making,
For ninety Moons-of-Gathering-of-Wild-Rice,
For ninety Moons-of-the-Falling-of-the-Leaves,
For ninety Moons-of-the-Coming-of-the-Snow.

STILL-DAY, THE MEDICINE-MAN

Mystic he was, more deep and passionless
Than a stagnant pond beneath a film of weeds;
But when the clouds went combering up the sky,
And Thunder-spirits, rumbling in the dusk,
Flickered their tongues of lightning ghastly green,
His withered lips would ripple with a prayer,
Like water-reeds before a gasp of wind.

Socketed deep among his bold bronzed features,
Worn dull from long communing with the ghosts
Of fish, of snakes, of moaning dead, his eyes
Held never a hint of evil; except in winter,
When bleak Kee-wáy-din, ghost-of-frozen-death,
Flung on a swirl of snow, from out a deep
Dark pocket of the night, a Great White Owl—
Ugh! Black-medicine! . . . beneath his lids
A stealthy soul would glint like any weasel
Gliding among the shadows in the rushes.
When Northern Lights came slipping from the cave
Of spirits in the land-of-winter-ice,
And lifted up a spectral hand to clutch
The shuddering stars—*Hi-yáh! Dark Mystery!*
Baleful and sinister the fleeting mood
That swept across his stoic countenance,
As when a black bat darts across the moon
And throws a flapping shadow on a pool.

MRS. DOWN-STARS

A Widow and Her Three Daughters:
Seraphine,
Josephine,
Josette.

O winter wind, move gently in this wood;
Here lives a gaunt black birch, so old, so worn,
So haggard with the snows of eighty winters
That nothing remains of her but tattered dreams,
And, sheltered by her withered arms, the fruit
Of an ancient ardor long since gone to dust:
Three saplings, shimmering-clean and cherry-red,
That loop the forest floor with supple limbs.

O winter storm, though here are three young dancers
Eager to make a high wild song of winds,
To leap upon the dust of yesterday,
There is a broken dreamer in this wood
Who knows no song except a requiem,
No step for dancing on a billowy snow-drift
Except the macaber click of hollow bones
And the shuffle of ghostly feet. O January,
Shake out no moan from her, and be no urge
To her unwilling feet; oh, let her sink
Gently to earth in her good time and season,
To dreams, to dreamlessness; and cover her,
Cover her softly with your drift of snow,
As tenderly as this gaunt birch let fall
Her leaves and bedded down her saplings three
Against the coming of a cold, cold winter.

CAMRON, THE INDIAN-TRADER

Camron, the trader, had a way with him,
A something in his thin white thread of lip
When bargaining with Indians he sought to beat
Them down in prices put on huckleberries,
With dubious talk of markets glutted, falling.
Niggard he was in the currency of speech.
Out of a cold white mouth his words would click
And clatter on the hardwood desk like coins;
And when he deigned to drop a word of barter,
Cold and metallic, the squaws would pick it up,
And—so to speak—would bite upon its edge
And fling it down upon a slab of stone,
Spinning and clinking, to find if it was good.

But every word he tossed them, good or specious,
The women soon or late would hold of worth;
When bellies are flat with hunger as a pike's
In spawning-season, any round glittering word,
Silver or leaden, soft between the teeth
Or brittle enough to nick a coyote's fangs—
If it but jingles faintly on a stone—
Falls on an Indian ear like silver music.

MR. AND MRS. PETER BIG-CLOUD

One day in every moon the Big-Clouds spent
In recreation at Fort Brule—or rite,
Perhaps would be more accurate, so solemn
It was and so unvaried in detail.
Three sleeps before the waning of the moon,
Old Peter and his palpably better half
Trudged with their heavy packs from out the hills
Down twenty twisted miles of rocky trail
And cranberry-bog. As straight as honey-bees
Wing to the bloom of their desire, they flew
To the Trading Post, and bartered there for tea
And pork their store of fur and maple-sugar.

After an endless argument on price
And quantity, involving frequent parleys
And digital arithmetic distressing
But accurate, so deliberate they were,
They capped the weighty enterprise of day
With a sparkling draught of magic soda-pop,
A beaded beverage more sweet and scarlet
Than dead-ripe thimbleberries, as glittering
With bubbles as a winter sky with stars—
A draught that tingled so mysteriously
Within one's nostrils, that one perforce must take
This highest moment of the month with vast
Discretion and all the high slow seriousness
That crises of such consequence demand.

Turning from sober fact, they plumped themselves
Upon the reed-rimmed shore of Bowstring Lake.
All afternoon they squatted among the rushes
And held communion with the lapping waves—
Or so it seemed; for never a muscle quivered,
Never a lip let fall a word in answer
To heckling foe or ingratiating friend.
Stolid they sat till dusk, like two huge frogs
Humped in the adder-docks that rim a pool;
Like monstrous bullfrogs idling in the sun,
Lethargic with comfort, blinking soberly,
And undisturbed by the buzz of bumblebees
Seeking to harry them to consciousness—
Nor even deigning to snap and swallow down
The dragon-flies—made bold by their apathy—
Dancing upon the islands of their noses.

BAZILE DEAD-WIND, THE BEGGAR

He squatted in the mud with hand outstretched,
Beetled of forehead, pocked and scrofulous,
Bulbous of scarlet nose; but with the stream
Of silver jingling in his birchen bucket,
The vagabond waxed somehow crimson-clean,
As a warty toadstool flushes into life
Beneath the benediction of cool sweet rain.

Upon his make-believe throne of basswood box
And tinseled calico, among his vermilion
War-drums, his clubs, and eagle-feather bonnets,
All day he held the marble of his posture:
Chief War-Hawk, Bloody Terror of the Sioux,
The foe of Custer.

                Before the gaping yokels
Caught by his tawdry art, and those who flung
An avalanche of jeers at him, he perched,
Open of lid, transfixed of countenance—
Kin to an owl that perches on a limb,
Gone blind with sunlight, blinking solemnly,
And unaware of the crowds of raucous blue jays
Chattering and ringed about him in excitement;
An owl that holds in the sockets of his eyes,
Through stolid sun, the beauty of a night
Gone into yesterday: a lonely pine
Leaning its tip upon the moon; the cool
Deep sough of wind among the sighing firs;
A far low quaver from the gloom; the blur
Of outspread wings that whistle down the wind
In a shy swift overture . . . two in the moonlight.

MRS. THUNDER-BEATER, THE WIDOW

On Independence Day she brought them all
To Fort McCullom—children as bewildered
And multitudinous as partridge chicks.
All day they gambled with catastrophe:
Little-Red-Bittern, swept beneath the trucks
Of rumbling artillery and under the wheels
Of the sudden-noise-on-wagons; Butterfly,
Beneath a cataract of prancing hoofs—
The mounts of pony-soldiers on parade;
Moon-Coming-Up, who scorched her cloud of hair
With jumping-fireworks; Yellow-Owl, who gorged
Himself to misery with frozen-creams,
Little-red-sugars, pickles, soda-pop.

All day the widow scurried around her brood
As any grouse in June that patters, frantic,
Clucking to all the lost, the lone, the bruised,
Battling with every eagle, owl, and hawk
That catapults from out the clouds to pounce
Upon her guileless bevy.

                    At last the moon,
Slipping its silver dollars through the lodge-peak,
Looked down upon the brood about a fire,
Slumbering, worn, at peace with Fort McCullom—
But for the one who sat awake, alert,
And inventoried all her roosting flock,
Counting her chicks by telling off each one

Upon the bony fingers of her hands,
And dreaming of a land of no forts,
No pony-soldiers, no sudden-noise-on-wagons,
No crazy-jumping-fire, no soda-pop.

INDIAN TRYST

Deep in a soundless grotto of the pines
Washed by the moon, she brooded—slim and cold
As an unlit candle waiting for the touch
Of eager flame to set its heart aglow,
Waiting to leap with life, and to consume
Itself with the ardor of a single night.

THE MISCREANT, ANGEL

Angel Cadotte was mischievous, more roguish
Than any chipmunk in a bin of oats.
But when the daily storm of wrath would break
After a prank upon the priest or teacher,
And justice—in the form of Michael Horse,
The reservation policeman—sought to lay
A rod of birch across his quivering back,
Angel would scurry to my side for refuge,
And cling tenaciously upon my legs
Until the storm had passed—as any woodsman,
Buffeted, beaten by tumultuous rains,
Seeks out the shelter of a thick-boughed fir,
And flattening himself against the trunk,
Clings to the bark with fingers desperate.

Oh, it was good to be a friendly fir-tree
Shielding a wild young body from the storm;
And good to feel the frenzied clutch of hands,
The cannonading of a wild young heart.

And if, in the fancy of a luckless wilding,
You were the only fir-tree in the world
That had a lee and overhanging boughs,
What would you do? And did you ever see
A tree, offended by some childish prank,
Fold up its branches? walk away in wrath?
And leave a little boy without a shelter
Against the beat of rain? Impossible!

TEAL-WING, A COUNCIL SPEAKER

Whenever Teal-Wing spoke in the council-ring,
He weighed his words in a manner of his own.
Cunning he was and cautious in each move—
With something of the spirit of a coyote
Loping through hostile, unfamiliar country.
He stepped like any wolf that skirts the fields
And holds to shadows, trotting a furlong or more—
Suddenly stopping to sniff the air with a tilted
Sensitive nose, to look, North . . . East . . .
South . . . West; jogging another furlong
Or more, and freezing again to catch the wind,
To look, North . . . East . . . South . . . West—
A tainted breeze! the smell of a man! a trap!—
And off with the wind in a wide circuitous path,
A long detour; and back again on the trail,
Trotting a furlong or more, with a pause to tilt
His nose, North . . . East . . . South . . . West.

On broncos loping down the asphalt street,
Behind a band that blared the Weary Blues,
They jogged—the stars of Buffalo Harry's Troupe:
Chief Scalping-Knife, on a drooping pinto mare,
And Mountain-Bird, astride a broomtail blue.

Stolid they seemed, like the cayuse mares they rode;
Yet theirs was but ironic listlessness.
For he of the pinto pony rode no mount
Of flesh, of mane, of piebald hide; his legs
Were wrapped about a lightning-flash that bucked
Among the crackling clouds and scraped the sky,
Crashing the while, for feet upon the earth,
Huge thunderbolts that left a flaming wake
Of death in all the cities in the land
Of bands, calliopes, and asphalt streets.
And he of the broomtail forked a thin blue wind
That streamed across the plains and cantered home:
Home to the teepees slumbering in the starlight
Beneath the slim blue smoke of burning pine;
Home to the valleys of the sky, so still,
Except for the muttering of moonlit brooks,
The friendly whinny of the winds, the faint
Far clank of hobble-chains on buckskins grazing
Deep in the meadows cool and crisp with frost.

TRAPS-THE-LIGHTNING, A HEADMAN

I told him where the tribal funds had vanished:
Seventeen-hundred irons, retaining-fee
For Daniel Clegg to represent the tribe
Among the Big-Knives; a hundred for the Mission;
Two thousand irons for the pilgrimage
To Washington to see the Chief-of-Big-Knives.
And as I spoke, his eyes locked fast with mine;
Over my heart I felt the slow sure beat
Of breakers cannonading up the sands,
Spreading among the crags with a quiet wash,
And feeling out among the crevices,
The secret caves, the grottoes of the dead,
With insinuating foamy fingers—searching,
Searching for something that they could not find.

PART XII

RED GODS

WEENG*

An Indian Slumber-song

Hush! my baby, or soon you will hear
The Sleepy-eye, Wéeng-oosh, hovering near;
Out of the timber he will come,
A little round man as small as your thumb.
Swinging his torch of a red fire-fly,
Out of the shadows old Sleepy-eye,
With the sound of a ghost, on the wind will creep
To see if a little boy lies asleep;
Over your cheeks old Weeng will go,
With feet as soft as the falling snow—
Tip-toe . . . . tip-toe.

Hush! my little one, close your lids tight,
Before old Sleepy-eye comes tonight;
Hi-yáh! if he finds you are still awake,
He draws from his quiver a thistledown stake;
With an acorn for club he pounds on its butt,
Till Sleepy-eye hammers the open eye shut;
Then from his bundle he pulls out another,
Hops over your nose and closes the other;
Up and down with his club he will rap
On the open lid till he closes the gap—
Tap-tap . . . . tap-tap.

If Wéeng-oosh comes at the end of this day,
And finds you asleep he will hurry away . . .

* For supplementary notes on "Weeng" and other poems in this
group, Part XII, see *Appendix*, page 356.

Do you hear him cry on the winds that blow?—
And walk on the earth as soft as a doe?—
To-and-fro . . . . to-and-fro . . .
Hi-yáh! he has crept away from my lap!
For he found my little boy taking a nap.
Oh, weep no more and whisper low,
I hear the feet of Sleepy-eye go—
Tip-toe . . . . tip-toe.

THE BIRTH OF WÁY-NAH-BO-ZHÓO

Long ago, in the hunting-moon
After the muskrat brought between his paws
From the bottom of the sea the piece of mud
That made the beginning of the earth,
There lived a Woman-Who-Was-a-Ghost.
Ho!—she was pretty, as pretty to look at
As a whistling swan, as shy and wild.
She was so beautiful and good
That even the old women of our tribe,
Whose tongues are sharp from too much talking
And clucking between their teeth,
Have nothing to say about her.

All day, all night,
The sun and moon would look at her
And long to put their hands on her;
But their medicine was not strong enough.
Even the big strong gods, the Thunder-bird,
The White Bear, the crafty Coyote,
Hungered for her; and every night
They tried to enter the woman's lodge
And lie down beside her until morning.

That is good to think about, my friend—
Ain't?—but for a younger man than I.

But every night they paced the woods,
Sucked in their breath, and ground their teeth;
For Grandmother Nóh-koh-mís, the Earth,

Circled the wéeg-i-wam all night
And guarded the pretty-one too well,
Like a dog that watches a buffalo-bone;
Grandmother Earth, with the sharp wet nose
And pointed ears of a fox with cubs,
Catching the scent of any sneaking lover,
The crackle of a twig beneath his feet,
Would snarl back her lips upon her teeth,
Shriek to the frightened stars,
And chase him back into the woods
With a big club of iron oak.

When I was a young man, my friend,
I could have given her a good run,
The old hag! No old woman could stop me;
There was no daughter I could not cover,
In the dark of the moon.

Among the lovers were the four windy spirits;
They were too cunning for old lady Nóh-koh-mís.

My son,
Women are women—
Even the best of them.

One night the Spirit-of-the-East-Wind
Crept from the Land-of-the-Morning-Sun;
Softly behind a fog that covered the hills
He stepped, on the still wet feet
Of a quiet little rain;
Softly he crept upon his belly

Into the pretty woman's lodge.
All night he lay beside her
And covered her face with wet kisses.

She did not move a muscle.
The blue sky in her dreams
Did not hold one blur—
Except a little cloud of gray.

He was very smart, my friend—ain't?
Rainy weather is always good for stalking.

Another night the Spirit-of-the-South-Wind,
Floating from the Land-of-Whip-poor-wills,
Came up the valley of the Big-River,
Crawled under the wéeg-i-wam wall
And stretched himself beside her.
With his fingers as soft and warm
As the breeze in the Moon-of-Flowers
He touched her breasts;
With a breath more sweet
Than the air in the Moon-of-Flowers,
When the chokecherry trees are full of blossoms,
He put his mouth to hers.
All night he breathed his sweet warm breath
On the pretty woman while she slept.

She did not move a muscle.
The blue sky in her dreams
Did not hold one blur—
Except a little cloud of yellow-green.

He is always smart with women—ain't?—
This windy-one. When he comes up the valley,
Always in spring, the women
Sing to themselves, sigh every minute,
And go walking all alone in the forest.
When I was a foolish little boy
There was a mystery in this;
But I learned something one day—
From a pair of squirrels;
And after that, when the south wind blew,
I would hide by the forest-trail,
And wait for the girls, and catch them.
They would not struggle much.
I am also smart—ain't?

Another night the Spirit-of-the-West-Wind
Danced on sure feet from the Land-of-Coyotes;
Until the moon swam down the sky
He hid himself among the spruces,
Sighed in the crowns of all the pines,
And made strong songs among the branches.
All evening he blew in the hollow river-reeds
And played upon them as if they were lovers'-flutes;
In the hour before the break of day
He came with dancing feet into the woman's lodge
And pulled her close to him.

She did not move a muscle.
The blue sky of her dreams
Did not hold one blur—
Except a little cloud of vermilion.

She was a heavy sleeper—ain't?—
Like mák-wa, the bear, who holes up
To sleep all winter—Ho!
But that is the way my grandfather told it,
And he knew everything about beginnings—
And his tongue could never talk crooked.

Another night the Spirit-of-the-North-Wind
Came roaring from the Land-of-Big-White-Bears.
Spitting and yelling among the lodge-poles,
With his icy hands he ripped the birch-bark
Flapping on the peak and dropped by the sleeper.
All night he crushed her to his ribs
With his big white twisted arms
And put his hard lips on hers.

She did not move a muscle,
Not even a finger, an eyelid.
The blue sky of her dreams
Did not hold one shadow—
Except a little cloud of white.

That is the way to take a woman—Ho!—
With noise, strong arms, and quick sharp teeth.
But each of the windy-spirits had a way
All his own, and every way was good.

One morning in the Moon-of-the-Suckers
The spirit-woman clapped her hands
Over her mouth; her eyes grew round and white;
For she was heavy with a child to come,

271

And felt a kicking out of legs.
And Nóh-koh-mís drew back her lips
Over her yellow teeth and smiled;
She knew that only a ghost, a spirit-one,
Could have dodged her eyes and tricked her,
Only a ghost could have been with the lovely-one.

In the Moon-of-Strawberries
The virgin dropped four children on the earth,
Beside a spring, and she was very glad.
One child was like the Spirit-of-the-East;
He had a very solemn face,
Wet eyes that never smiled,
And very quiet hands and feet.
One child was like the Spirit-of-the-South,
Sighing all day and humming softly—
His hands were soft and warm.
One child was like the Spirit-of-the-West,
With quick tough feet,
And a wide big-singing mouth.
One child was like the Spirit-of-the-North—
Bellowing every minute, full of tricks,
And always kicking out with arms and legs.

The four strong windy-ones stretched up
And grew more swiftly than corn-stalks
Fed by much rain and sun;
After forty sleeps they stood
Much taller than their mother—
Ho! bigger than tall smokes.

At sunset, early in the Moon-of-Falling-Leaves,
While their mother was kneeling by a spring,
Filling her birch-bark buckets,
The windy brothers huddled together
In a thicket of bent balsams
And whispered strange things to one another.
Quickly they parted, ran in four directions,
And wheeled to face their kneeling mother.
Together they drew deep breaths,
Puffed out their cheeks together,
And together blew upon the woman—
Big gusts that swirled around her,
That stripped the trees of all their leaves,
And flung a whirling cloud of dust on her.

When the dust and leaves had settled,
And the roaring winds had fallen to a whisper—
Like going thunder after a summer-storm—Ho!—
Nobody, nobody was bending by the spring;
The spirit-woman had vanished from the world,
Like a snow-flake before a sudden sultry wind—
Nobody knows to what strange country
Of spirit-ones she went, nobody can say.

She did not leave one track, one sign,
To show that she had walked this earth—
Except beside the spring a round red spot
Upon the soil where she had given birth
To her four windy children.

On the crimson spot upon the dirt—
As a pine that sends its roots into the soil

From a little seed, and moon by moon,
Stretches itself and reaches to the sky—
So Wáy-nah-bo-zhóo, the mischief-maker,
Fastened himself on earth and grew;
From the crimson spot upon the ground,
Nourished by seven summers of sun and rain
And the milk-dripping breast of Nóh-koh-mís,
Wáy-nah-bo-zhóo drew up his mighty body;
For seven summers more and seven winters
His windy brothers fed him, trained him every day
For jumping, fighting, cunning,
And blessed him with their powers:
Child-of-the-East-Wind built in him
The calmness of rain, still feet for stalking,
And the mystery of quiet-falling rain;
Child-of-the-South-Wind put in him
A warm heart, a tongue for soft sweet talk,
And hands that could be very gentle;
Child-of-the-West-Wind shaped his mouth
For many bright songs, his limber legs
For dancing easily and steadily;
Child-of-the-North-Wind made in him
The strong white bones of winter,
Big shoulders that could crack an oak
As if it were a withered reed,
And put upon his iron lips
The sounding words of blizzards.

What man of blood and bone, my son,
Can wrestle with a child of the four winds?
And of a woman who was a ghost?—

274

Or talk more big and strong than he?
  Or play more tricks?
  Or be more smart?
  Or more mysterious?
    Nobody . . .
    Nobody . . .

CHANT FOR THE MOON-OF-FLOWERS

On the sacred flame, O Mighty Mystery,
I fling my handful of good red willow bark;
Like willow smoke that floats upon the dusk,
My prayer goes winding up the sky to you:

In the Moon-of-Strawberries-and-Raspberries
Stain the green world, O Maker-of-all-good-things,
With a bursting yield of berries; let them hang
Plenty upon the bush, and heavy with blood.
Let the trout and whitefish walk into my nets
Thick as the stars that swim across the sky;
And may the Big-Knives offer plenty silver
For every catch of fish; ho! let the price
Of fat young pike and trout be seven coppers
No longer—eight is good, and nine is better.
    Not for myself I ask all this,
      But for my little boy, Red-Owl,
          For he is good.

In the Moon-of-Blueberries ask our mother earth
To let the sap go up her stalks of corn
In sparkling currents; make the huckleberries
So plentiful that when we shake the twigs
Above the mó-kuk, the sagging fruit will patter
Down on the birch-bark bucket—round blue rain;
Make the wild hay deep among the meadows,
More soft and thick than winter-fur of beaver,
So thick the north wind cannot part the grasses.

Not for myself I ask these presents,
But for my daughter, Little-Bee,
    For she is good.

In the Moon-of-Changing-Color-of-the-Leaves
Ripen the wild rice growing in the marshes,
Until the yellow grains are full of milk,
Ripe for the world, like heavy-breasted women;
In the wet mush-káigs, make cranberries plentiful,
Thick as the dots that mark the spotted trout;
And may the goose-plums on the tree be many,
So full of clear red honey that they burst
Their skins and spatter sweet upon the earth.
    Not for myself I ask these gifts,
    But for my woman, Yellow-Wing,
        For she is good.

Ho! Mystery, I fling upon the fire
My handful of willow bark to make you glad;
Open your hands and toss me many presents
Showering on the earth like falling leaves.

I

Hó-yo-hó-ho! . . . . yo-ho!
Wáy-nah-bo-zhóo, big spirit of our Brother,
Come thou and bless us, for the maple flows,
And the Moon-of-Sugar-Making is upon us.
The nights are white with frost; the days are yellow
With sunshine; and now the sap of the maple-tree,
Humming the sugar-song, goes up the stem
With dancing feet. The gabbling geese come tumbling
Out of the wind and into the wet mush-káig
In clattering families; among the reeds
The fat old women-geese go chattering
Of winter-lands; and gathered on the shore,
Shouting with hearts glad to be home again,
The goose-men strut in council, and flutter and snort.
Ah-chée-dah-mó, the spluttering tail-up squirrel,
Pokes his blue whiskers from his hole in the oak,
And scurries up and down the swaying branches—
He runs in six directions, all over the earth,
Hurrying, looking everywhere for somebody,
Something he cannot find—nor does he know
Why the green wet days should be so bitterly sweet.
Ho! the yellow-birch throbs, for she knows the pain of life,
Of swelling limbs and bursting buds; she stands
With naked arm stretched out to the warm gray rains,
With hungry arms that tremble for her lover,
For Sée-gwun, the Maker-of-little-children, who comes
With soft blue feet that rustle the fallen leaves.

Hear thou the maple-water dripping, dripping,
The cool sweet-water dripping upon the birch-bark.
Ho! the Moon-of-Sugar-Making is upon us!

Hó-yo-hó-ho! . . . . yo-ho!
Hear thou our prayers, O Brother, Wáy-nah-bo-zhóo!
Hear, thou who hast made the flat green earth for us
To dance upon, who dost fold us in thy hands
Tenderly as a woman holds a broken bird
In winter, thou our Brother who hast hung the sun
Upon the sky to give us warmth and life,
And the wet moon to make us cool and clean;
Hear, thou who hast made the hills and the timber-beasts
That roam them, who hast made the sliding rivers
And silver fish that shiver in the pools—
That there might be wild meat for empty bellies;
Hear, thou who hast made cold rapids in the canyons,
Wild waterfalls, and springs in the cool green hollows—
That there might be sweet water for parching tongues;
Hear, thou who hast given us thy mother, All-Mother Earth,
That she might feed her children from her bosom—
Ah-yee! Wáy-nah-bo-zhóo, come thou on this night
With blessings as the maple-water flows;
Make thou a song to our heavy-breasted mother,
And pray thou that her children may not hunger,
For now is the night for maple-sugar feasting.

Hó-yo-hó-ho! . . . . yo-ho!
From the long cold of winter moons, our eyes
Are deep, our hands like the bundled veins and talons
Of buzzard birds. Before the winter winds

279

The moose have run to other lands for feeding;
The rabbits have vanished as the snow—a plague
Left a strange red sickness in their withered mouths.
Even old Gahg, the clumsy porcupine,
No longer finds his way to our roasting-pots—
We boil his yellow bone-ribs many times—
Ugh! our teeth grow soft without strong meat to eat.

Ho! Wáy-nah-bo-zhóo, hear thou our many tears
Dropping among the dead leaves of winter;
Pray thou, and ask our grandmother, Waking-Earth,
To take us in her arms, to make us warm
With food, to hold us safe upon her bosom.
Our mouths go searching for her mighty breasts,
Where the maple-milk comes flowing from the trees—
Ah-yee! Brother, pray thou now the Mother-One
To give us freely of her sugar-sap,
The good sweet water of her bursting breasts—
For the Moon-of-Sugar-Making is upon us.
Hó-yo-hó-ho! . . . . yo-ho!

II

And if the sap flows thin with water, our hearts
Will hold no bitterness; for we shall know
That long ago in thy wisdom thou didst decree
That our mother's milk might never be too thick—
Fearing that we should gather plenty sugar
With little labor and soon grow sick with food
And slow to move our legs, like glutted bear.
Ho! we are a faithful children of the soil;

We work with eager hearts and patient hands.
And if our birchen baskets crack and leak
The gathered sap, our tongues will speak no evil;
We know that thou, our Brother, in thy love
For all the Otter-tails, didst whip the growing
Birch-tree until the bark was cracked and cut
With round black stripes—that our birchen pails might leak
The golden sap, that thus all Indian children,
Laboring long with many steps, might never
Grow soft and fat with idling in the bush.
Ho! we are a faithful children of the soil;
We toil with eager hearts and patient backs.

Hi! Wáy-nah-bo-zhóo! Hear thou, O mighty one,
Who dost fold us in his tender hands as a woman
Holding a broken bird in the winter wind,
Come thou and bless us on this night of feasting.
Pray thou our mother to take us in her arms,
To hold us warm upon her great brown bosom,
To give us freely of her maple-water,
The good sweat water of her swelling breasts.
And if we labor long, our lips will speak
No bitterness, for our arms are strong for hauling,
Eager for many buckets of sweet sap,
For syrup dancing its bubbles up and down
In the kettles, to the bubble-dancing song.
Ho! for we are a faithful children of the soil;
We toil with trusting hearts and patient fingers—
And now is the Moon-of-Maple-Sugar-Making.
Hó-yo-hó-ho! . . . . yo-ho!

SPOTTED-FACE, THE TRIBAL FOOL, PRAYS

O Mystery, take my feast of maple-sugar
Set on this medicine-earth for you to eat!—
And let your heart grow good to me with presents.

Give me the legs and sinews of the moose,
For trailing otters steadily from sleep
To sleep; the cunning of the timber-wolf,
That I may kill prime fishers, minks, and martens;
And put upon the pan of my trap the paws
Of silver foxes, and let its ragged teeth
Hold to the bone with the never-ending clutch
Of quicksand—ho! many foxes—eleven, twelve!

All this I ask, that I may pack much fur
To the village—pelts to the muzzle of my gun,
Pelts that will put white eyes in the heads of all
The pretty-colored women, bold round eyes
That burn my spotted face with naked asking.

Put in my hands your devil-magic herbs:
A medicine to kill Blue-Whooping-Crane,
Whose pretty talk, like the tongue of a rattlesnake,
Tickled my woman until she bared her breast
To it and took his poison in her blood;
A medicine to wither and rot the legs
Of Pierre La Plante, who took her to his lodge,
And ran with her to parish Trois Pistoles.

Give me an herb to lock the jaws of women
Tight as a rusty trap, to freeze the lips

Of the dry old women of my tribe who speak
My name with mouths that flow with dirty laughter.

Fix me a woman, a woman who will hold
Herself for me alone, as the trumpeter-swan
That waits through lonely silver nights for wings
That whistle down the wind like an old song.

Ho! Mighty-Spirit, let your heart grow good
To me with presents; so much I ask—no more.

FEAST FOR THE MOON-OF-BREAKING-SNOWSHOES

CHIEF TWO-MOONS SPEAKS

My people, now is the time when trouble
Falls from our shoulders like the blanket
Of night that slips from the hills at daybreak;
Now is the time for the laughing of children.
The warm sweet-smelling breath of the wind
From the Land-of-Whip-poor-wills has blown
The melting snow to little ribbons;
The arbutus blossoms lift their heads
From the dead leaves and look around;
Seeing that all the sky is blue
And all the earth is full of milk,
Their faces grow pleasant with many smiles—
   For now is the Moon-of-Breaking-Snowshoes.

Mák-wa, the droll lean-bellied bear,
Comes rumbling from his winter den;
Clawing the earth for the rain-swollen roots
Of adders'-tongues, and stretching out
Among the ferns on the sunny hillside,
He grunts, for he is very glad.
The birds, the flowers, the budding trees,
Are beginning to talk to one another
And laugh quietly together—
   For now is the Moon-of-Breaking-Snowshoes.

II

BLACK-EAGLE, THE MEDICINE-MAN, CHANTS

O Mystery, for holding my struggling people
Warm in your hands through the bitter winter-moons,
      My heart is good to you.

For putting the paws of many minks and beavers
Into our traps and making thick prime fur,
      My heart is good to you.

For driving out the evil-spirit who drew
A stream of blood from the lungs of my little boy,
      My heart is good to you.

For washing the spotted-plague from my little girl
And painting her cheeks with thimbleberry juice,
      My heart is good to you.

For making my woman fat with another child
To fill our cradle with many arms and legs,
      My heart is good to you.

For the plenty sugar-sap that drips from the maples
When woodpeckers tap the trunks in the early morning,
      My heart is good to you.

For the plenty mallards we can hear each evening
Shouting together, glad to be home again,
      My heart is good to you.

HANDS-OVER-THE-SUN SPEAKS

Go now, my people, to your lodges;
Come back with presents for the spirits.
To those who give with one small hand
But hold back with the other,
The spirits also will be small . . .

Ho! Mrs. Big-Wolf's heart is good.
Look!—the crazy-quilt she draws
From beneath her shawl so cheerfully!
The moonlight that falls on windy water
Is not so beautiful to look at.
This woman needs no quilt to keep
The cold from her; her heart is warm . . .

Ho! Charging-Hawk throws down his snuff
On the blanket. Ugh! Only two boxes!
Too little—Ho!—is better than none . . .

Old Mrs. Rattling-Seeds, the widow,
Asks me to speak to you for her:
To end her year of lonely mourning
She offers a feast when the sun sinks;
Four iron kettles full of soup
With plenty venison and wild rice
To make it good; and porcupines—
Roasted, she says, and four of them;
Plenty tobacco for the men,
New maple-sugar for the women,

And red-round-sours for the children.
Come with your buckets for the soup.

Ho! I—and my plenty family—
Will be among the first to come.
And I will be the first to dance
With her. Widow, beware of me!

THE CONJURER

Come ye, spirits three!
Out of the East, out of the West, out of the North!
Rise ye, má-ni-dó, from your wéeg-i-wams
In the corners of the earth!
Blow, blow, blow thy raging tempests
Through the ranks of whining pine!
Come ye! Come ye to my chée-sah-kán
Riding on thy crazy-running winds.
Hear! Hear my potent chantings!
Bestow me the strength to work my conjurings.
Hi! Take ye my good medicine,
This precious skin of a jumping-rat
Killed in the hour when death,
When clattering death walked into my lodge—
And three moons, three moons dried
On the grave of my youngest son.
Hi! Hear me! Hear me, má-ni-dó!

Come ye, spirits three!
Out of the East, out of the West, out of the North!
Hi! Blow, blow, blow thy whirling winds!
Sway my wéeg-i-wam, sway it
With the breathings of the cyclone!
Hi! Bend its birchen poles
Like the reeds in yonder bay!
Hi! Clutch my wéeg-i-wam, bend it
Till its peak shall scrape the ground!
Hear me! Hear me, má-ni-dó!

How! How!
Behold! my friends, it bends
Like a lily in the storm!

Come ye, spirits three!
Out of the East, out of the West, out of the North!
On the wings of the wind send into my lodge
The lean spirit of a lean coyote—
Of the dying prairie-wolf whose whimperings
We followed many sleeps across the desert.
Make him, má-ni-dó, fling up again
His last long mournful wailings
When thirst and hunger clutched
His withered aching throat—
That the old men of my tribe may hear
Again his ghostly callings as of old.
Hear me! Hear me, má-ni-dó!

How! How!
Ho! There is a power
In my precious ratskin!

Come ye, spirits three!
Out of the East, out of the West, out of the North!
On the wings of the wind send into this lodge
The spirit of Sings-in-the-Hills
Who walked to his death in his birch canoe
Over the falls of the Cut-Foot Waters.
Blow his spirit into my lodge,
That his aged father who sits without
May hear his voice again.

Hear me! Hear me, má-ni-dó!
Make his ghost to talk from my lodge
That the people who watch my juggling
May know his voice again.

How! How!
Hear, my people?
My medicine-skin is strong with power!

Hear ye, spirits three!
Go ye back to thy wéeg-i-wams
In the corners of the earth.
Into the East, into the West, into the North.
Leash again the wolves of the wind. . . .
To thee, O Má-ni-dó of the East,
This handful of burning balsam
Which I fling on the dying wind;
To thee, O Má-ni-dó of the West,
This handful of yellow medicine,
Powder of precious clays;
To thee, O Má-ni-dó of the North,
This red willow twig whereon I have rubbed
My potent medicine ratskin.
Go ye back, ye má-ni-dó,
To the corners of the earth!
Hah-eeee-yóooooooooooo!

How! How!
Enter ye the wéeg-i-wam, my friends!
Unbind ye the basswood cords from my body!
I am done!
How! How!

RAIN SONG

I

God of the Thunders, Thunder-God,
Hear thou our medicine-rattles!
Hear! Hear our sounding drums!
Hi! Our medicine-bag on yonder rock
Has a power, a big-good medicine power—
Three silver scales of the Great Sea Monster—
Ho! Big rain-medicine! Strong rain-medicine! Ho!
Ugh! Behold! On the rock by the stream the Beast
Has placed three scales from his slimy belly—
Ho! Big medicine! Ho! Strong medicine!—
Silver scales of the Big Sea Monster!
Hi! Spirit-of-Thunder, come in thy fury,
Come with thy wet winds, come with thy many waters;
Come in thy wrath against thy foe
That taunts thee there with his filthy poison.
All the children of the earth are good,
Heap-good in the heart to the Thunders;
All the children of the earth are bitter—
Ugh!—bitter to thy foe, the Demon!
We spit!—Behold! we spit on him!
Come with a heart that is good to thy children—
Ho! And big-many waters and heap-much rain!
Come with a heart that is bad to our enemy—
Ho! And big-much lightning, plenty-big storm!
Ho! Silver-wing God, with thy swift wet feet,
Come! Come! Come in thy big black war clouds!
Hurl thy arrows of flashing flame!

Rush at our foe with thy whirlwind waters!
Crush with thy storms the stinking beast
That defies thee here with his slimy poison—
Ho! Big medicine! Ho! Strong medicine!—
Silver scales of the Big Sea Snake!

Ho!

II

Hah-yée! Hah-yó-ho-o-o-o! Hah-yó-ho-o-o-o!
God of the Thunders, Thunder-God,
Hear thou our medicine-rattles!
Hear! Hear our sounding drums!
Two moons the mountain brooks have been dry,
And the panting birds like ghosts in a row,
Perch in the shade and sing no longer.
Our Brother, the Sun, can find his face
No more in the shining-glass of the river;
His eyes see nothing but yellow cracked mud
As wrinkled as the skins of our old women.
Eagerly the sunflower lifts her mouth to the dew,
Yet her lips parch and her head droops,
And her leafy arms grow thin and wither.

Ai-yee! Thunderer, Spirit of the Big Waters,
With burning tongues all the children of the earth—
The flower-people and the hungry grasses,
The sky-flyers and the water-walkers—
All, all are calling, calling, calling to thee.
Hear! Hear our many, many callings!
Hah-yée! Hah-yó-ho-o-o-o! Hah-yó-ho-o-o-o!

Thick with hot dust the old men of the forest
Stand with bended heads complaining wearily,
Grumbling ever at the hot winds,
Mumbling ever of the beating sun.
Among the brittle pines the fires run
With many swift feet through the crackling bushes;
And the deer, like whirling leaves in the wind,
Scurry madly before their scorching breath.
The sweet wet grass of our valley-meadows
Is blown by the hot winds into powder;
And our ponies nibble at rustling rushes.
Like the papoose that puts its mouth
To the scrawny breast of an old squaw,
The corn thirstily sucks at the earth—
In the blistered earth there is dust, dust.
And my brothers talk with thick hot tongues,
And my people walk with skinny bellies,
And die like the burning grass of the prairies.

Ai-yee! Thunderer, Spirit of the Big Waters,
With parching mouths all the children of the earth—
The many-foot-walkers and the belly-creepers,
The timber-beasts and the all-over-the-earth-walkers—
All, all are calling, calling, calling to thee.
Hear! Hear their many, many callings!
Hah-yée! Hah-yó-ho-o-o-o! Hah-yó-ho-o-o-o!

III

Háh-yaaaaaaah! Háh-yaaaaaaah!
Háh-yaaaaaaah! Háh-yaaaaaaah!

God of the Thunders, Thunder-God,
Hear thou our medicine-rattles!
Hear! Hear our sounding drums!
Hí-yee! Behind the clouds on the far horizon,
Beat, beat, beat on thy crashing war-drums!
Hí! Hi! Hí! To the war-dance beat,
Shake the earth with thy stamping feet!
Over the fires of the blazing sky
Fling thy blankets of thick wet mist.
Roll from the hills the wet gray fog.
Blow from the hills the cool wet winds.

Hi! Come! Come! Come, thou God of the Thunder!
Come on thy whirling winds from the West!
Come with a rush of thy wings of silver!
Crush our foe with thy tramping feet!
Hí! Hi! Hí! With thy flame-plumed war-club,
Crack the skies in wrath asunder;
And pour from thy hands through thy silver fingers
Cool sweet-waters on the panting earth.
Ho! Wingèd-One of the rumbling rain clouds,
With thy war-drums, sky drums, call thy Water-Spirits.
On thy serpent-foe—we spit on him!—
Let loose thy fire-flashing Thunder.
Ho! Big Tornado! Ho! Thou Cyclone!
Rouse from slumber, dash from the North!
Ho! Big Hand-Walker, who goes head down,
With twirling legs that walk in the sky,
Come over the plains with thy trailing hair
Of tangled winds and twisting rains.

294

Ho! Thou God of the Thunder-drums,
Pour from thy hands the many-many waters:
Ho! Rains like clouds of silver lances,
Cool long rains that slant from the West;
Rains that walk on gentle little moccasins,
Softly slipping from the fogs in the East;
Cold white rains from the Land-of-Winter,
Dripping in the trees, beating on the birch-bark;
Soft rains, gray rains, rains that are gentle,
Swift rains, big rains, rains that are windy—
Rains, rains, many-many rains.

Hi! Thou God of the Sounding Thunder,
Split the clouds with thy club asunder!
Come! Come! Come with thy stamping feet!
Hí! Hi! Hí! To the war-dance beat!
Bitter in the heart to the Great Sea Monster;
Bitter to our foe; bitter to his poison—
Ho! Big medicine! Ho! Strong medicine!
Silver scales of the Big Sea Snake!

Ho! Ho!

MEDICINE-MAN CONVERSATIONALLY TO THE ASSEMBLED
   TRIBE:

Go to thy wéeg-i-wams, my people.
Already the morning star is high.
Sleep with untroubled hearts.

Come tomorrow to the dancing-ring;
The doctors will then dance the Thanks-Song.
Bring presents—Ho!—and plenty meat!

Ugh! Lame-Wolf! . . . Tobacco! . . .
Ugh! . . . I spit on your red willow tobacco!
It has no teeth! It is for squaws!
Give me your white man's tobacco—
The black stick with the stuck-on silver dog! . . .

PART XIII

LUMBERJACKS AND VOYAGEURS

FOX-HEART

Any November storm in Pointe du Loup
Will drive a coyote slinking to his den;
But I had never seen such an avalanche
Of elements combine to barricade
The world with ice, as on the biting night
That heralded the winter of five-foot snow.
Such cosmic din!—the pine-trees split of heart
And bellowing with pain; the keen-toothed wind,
Spitting beneath the eaves like a frozen cat,
And scratching on the sashes of the windows.

In all the sea of tossing wilderness
Our logging-camp was like a friendly light-house.
Banked round the roaring bunk-house stove—so hot
That it could pop a chestnut to the rafters—
The men were bent on drowning out the gale
With thump of hobnailed boot, and red-lunged laughter:
Perched on a keg, the bull-cook, Jacques Mineau,
Was tuning up his fiddle; at his side,
McCandless fingered his accordion;
Pawing each other, maneuvering into place,
The shantymen, grown rosy with good gin,
Were shouting for a reel . . .

Promenade all!—

We heard a timid knocking at the door;
Merely the wind, we thought, upon the panel,
Tapping its sleeting fingers . . .

Allamen right!—

Again we heard a knocking at the door,
A scratching on the pine, as if a cat,
A homeless cat, were trying to get in.
We flung aside the bar, and on the threshold,
Sleety from crown to toe, two spindling urchins
Tottered and almost fell; the half-breeds—twins—
Whimpered and queried us with eyes as bright
As buttons on a shoe—like little foxes
That stumble in the night upon a den
Of bears and, whining, squat before the hole.

We let them in. As straight as wildings trot
To find a dusky corner in a room,
They scurried to the wood-box by the stove
And burrowed in the logs; nor could we coax
Them out, so shy and wild their Indian hearts—
Till Swamper Jack, who always had a way
With women and children, with homeless cats and dogs,
Wheedled them out with monstrous bowls of stew,
A steaming mulligan. And while they lapped,
We set about to find a name for them,
For something told us they had come to stay—
And whatever loiters in a logging-camp
Must answer to a call. After hot talk,
We baptized them, with the shanty's oldest rye:
One, Demi John, the other, Jimmie John—
They were no taller than a jug of rum.

Their story came at last, with fitful jerks
Of Chippewa pidgin-talk: the squawman father
Gone with the Big-Knives' Sickness-on-the-lungs;

Nobody left, except the shattered squaw,
To rustle food for the undernourished nestlings;
And when at night the last blue wisp of spirit
Slipped from her flesh and vanished down the wind—
Leaving the two alone, and full of fear—
The children stumbled down the dark and came
Upon the logging-camp. We gleaned no more,
Except that life had been as cruel to them
As any heel to a family of ants.

And so we sheltered them. Somehow they brought
New spirit to the loggers, something to talk
About, to gambol with on snowed-in nights.
Oh, it was good to see the granite hearts
Of shaggy-breasted brutes go crumbling to soil
Beneath the touch of twenty copper fingers,
Yielding at last a root-hold for the blossom
Of warm compassion.

                    But it would tax a man
To put his hands upon the twins, so wary
And timid they were—so Indian-like. At first
They rarely ventured from behind the stove
Where Swamper Jack had bedded them with quilts;
They squatted on the birch like little foxes
Sunning themselves upon a hillock, drowsy,
Alert of ear with every sudden sound,
Scampering off at every sudden gesture.

With the cycle of the winter-moons they lost
Much of their Indian quiet. Antoine taught

301

The pair to shuffle up the floor in jigs,
That stuttered with his old accordion.
Geoffrey Beaudette, who owned one yellow tooth—
Scurvy and fights had wiped out all the others—
Set out to make life pleasant for the two
By coaching them in the art of chewing snuff.
The walking-boss gave up his nights of leisure
To teach them English—of a dubious nature;
Jeremy's chest would swell when they poured out
In treble tones a waterfall of words,
Pungent, malodorous as angry skunks—
Refinements of imprecation that Charbonneau
Had learned on his drunken evenings of romance
Among the frowsy cats of Trois Rivières.

Although their wild hearts yielded day by day
To the woodsmen's awkward friendliness, the two
Rarely forsook their cave of piled-up logs
Behind the fire, their refuge in the shadows.
Each night, when Jacques, the bull-cook, made the rounds
To snuff the lights and feed the stove with fuel,
He found the two rolled snug within the den,
Like cublets burrowed in a dusky hole,
Dozing with one black eye low-lidded, open
To every flash of match and flicker of candle.

In a playful mood one night I strove to lift
Them from their ragged covers while they slept.
Into their deep dark hole I shoved my arms;
My fingers thrilled to the velvet warmth of cheeks
Buried among the folds, the rise and fall

302

Of bellies round and marble-hard with food.
I clutched their rumps and tried to drag them out;
Startled from sleep, they fastened on the logs
And wriggled like angleworms that cling to a hole
And squirm from out one's fingers. I reached for them
Again—a snarl, a whimper, then at last
A very storm of feet and clawing hands,
Of tooth and toe and nail! I let them rest.
Somehow my thought went back a year to the spring
When I went hunting foxes, with the hope
Of selling all the whelps that I might catch
Alive to Angus Camron for his fur-ranch.

One day I tracked a red fox to her hole;
Plugging the burrows, I began to dig
My way and follow down the winding tunnels,
Driving ahead of me the litter of cubs
From pit to pit, until I cornered them
At last in one deep chamber. There they huddled,
Trembling with fright—the vixen had disappeared.
I tried to lift them with my naked hands
And put them in the pine-crate one by one.
Bitter that moment! The arm that groped along
The silken black of burrow, suddenly cringed
Beneath the slash of furious claws, the grip
Of needle-pointed jaws, and came up gashed
And running with a dozen crimson rivers!
It flashed on me that I had come a month
Too late for trapping, that foxlets in the spring
May grow sharp teeth with the passing of a moon . . .

And thus it dawned on us, the two-John boys
Truly were foxes, and growing foxes, too.

Starting one day at sunrise for the pines,
Where I had planned to swamp the trail, I felt
A subtle coming spirit in the woods,
A pungence in the air like rotting cedar
And old wet leaves turned over by the wind—
A stirring, faint, as if the muffled hills
Were coming out of death and into life.
I knew that I should see by night the thaws
Of spring set in.

       At noon the jam of ice
Broke and went out, and tossed upon a freshet.
The forest was alive with yellow flickers;
Hammering upon their maple drums, they loosed
A hundred silver runnels down the trunks.
Deep in the wintergreen, upon a knoll
Blown free of snow, I came upon a bud
Pushing its frail pink petals through the leaves
And reaching for the sunlight—the first arbutus
Breaking the winter-torpor of the hills
With color of life and fragrance of the earth.
And I was glad for this—the stir of life,
The promise of companionship tomorrow.
Month upon month of labor in a land
Of snow-crowned stumps like leaning drifted grave-stones,
A solitude forlorn with stark gray ghosts
That crouch among the snowy-hooded balsams,
Breeds in the heart a hunger for the sound

Or sign of any pulsing growing thing—
A bird, a bee, a palpitating bud.
And so thrice welcome was the splash of paw
I found upon a patch of tattered snow—
The scrawl of bears fresh out of winter-den.

That night there was less bedlam in the cabin—
A little talk about the jam of logs
Hung up at Split-rock, a fragmentary word
About the drive, the scaler's escapades
In Trois Rivières. And when a flock of geese,
Flapping against the silver of the moon,
Bugled their wild free music on the wind,
And coyotes answered, a spirit fell on us,
A mood mysterious and vaguely pregnant.
We felt it, even the boys, who seemed more wary,
More restless, more disposed to show their teeth
If anybody tried to nuzzle them.

At last the candles sputtered and went out.
We fell asleep, within our hearts the faint
Far echoes of a wolf among the hills,
A lonely coyote baying at the moon,
Calling to all the slumbering silver world,
Calling to every pricked-up silver ear.

When pale pink morning slanted five o'clock
Among the frosted spruce, and stirred Belile
To bellow his "Daylight in the swamp! Roll out!"
And to jangle us from bunk to breakfast-board,
We bolted for the drying-racks to get

305

Our socks and boots, and huddled at the stove
To break the morning chill. While we were bustling,
Tony LeBanion whirled upon the wood-pile:

"Wak' up! Sauvages! You hear those crazy cook
She's ring those bell!—no?"

                              He hurled a shoe-pac
Across the room; its exclamatory thump
Upon the log-box punctuated his sentence.
No sound came back to us.

                              "Sacré de Dieu!
Might be those boys she's dead from sleeping!—no?"

He tiptoed to the pile and plunged his arm
Deep in the hole to drag them out of sleep—
Only to lift to light a clutch of quilts
Bedraggled, frayed; the cairn of logs was empty,
Cold as a long-deserted foxes' den;
The Johnny-boys had vanished with the night,
The trumpeting geese, the shadows in the moon.
Nor did we grieve, or spend much time in talk
Beyond a grunt; we had foreseen this day,
Knowing as woodsmen, as kinsmen of the earth,
That when the sap goes sparkling up the stems
Of maple-trees and the homing snow-geese call
Across the dusk, the wild heart must answer—
That foxes must be foxes.

                              But when November
Tapping its sleety fingers on the roof,
And moaning dolefully among the pines,

Comes out of night and finds us at the fire,
A knocking, any little sound—a scratching
Upon the sash—will bring us to our feet.

And when December stars the vault of night
With incandescent ice, and the snow-dust creaks
And crunches under foot, and not a sound
Shivers the hollow air, the hollow sky—
Never a word is uttered, never an oath,
Or song to break the spell upon the crew—
Until a something in the starlight knocks
Upon the window; we fling aside the door,
Always—to let the frozen wind come in.

FIVE PEAS ON A BARREL-HEAD

The warden spoke of him as "Ninety-four,
The Mystery," and swore no man could plumb
His murky depths, his thinking. The prisoners,
Shunning him always for his sullenness,
Dubbed him "the loco Finn," and they would mutter
Stark tales of Waino's brawls in logging-camp—
Of the autumn night when Waino, swaggering,
Reeling with rot-gut gin, gone berserker,
Lifted his ax and split three heads wide open
As pretty as a knife could cleave three apples.
That drunken hour forever shut from him
The bounding sweep of Lake Superior's blue,
The surge and lapse of breakers on her crags,
The dulcet talk of rambling brooks and pines
Marching upon her shores.

                                    Little enough
There was about the Finnish lumberjack
To show the hot black lava in his breast.
Power he radiated, from his fists,
Iron and gnarled, his huge gorilla arms,
The granite of his block of head set square
And squat upon his bulging granite shoulders;
But power unfired, stagnant as a ditch.
Never a gleam lit up his slate-gray eyes.
His broad flat face was as shallow as a plate,
As empty of emotion. And when one dusk
He crept away and clambered to the roof
Of the heating-plant, catapulted himself

Flat on the air like any flying-squirrel,
Clutched at a cable and scrambled down its length
Hand over hand till he crossed the prison-wall
And there dropped twenty feet to earth, to dash
For the freedom of the hills—only to crumple
Under the slugs that whistled from the towers—
The desperado took our breath away.

"To think the stolid Finn," cried Hobbs, the warden,
"Could hold a hunger terrible enough
To breed such recklessness!" He shrugged his arms.
"And yet a black bear sleeping in his den
Seems droll enough and harmless; but who can say
When bears will run amuck and gut a township."

For this they clamped the logger in solitary,
And later in the warehouse, in cellar-gloom.
Here, where the stone walls dripped with chilly slime
And melancholy, month on month the Finn
Shifted his bales and boxes, rolled his barrels;
Burrowing underground like a sightless mole
Month upon month, he brooded and fell to bone
And pallid flesh.

        Regiments of mice
Began to levy on his sacks of barley,
His prunes, his corn and peas. MacDonald flung
A dozen traps before the blinking Finn
And told him to make an end of all the rodents.
Furtively Waino tucked the string of traps
Under his cot and never set a spring.

Something he liked about the squealing mice,
Something about their merrymaking, their sharp
And gusty delight in the high affairs of mice;
Something—somehow they brought him lively news
Of the pregnant earth six feet beyond the walls
They tunneled under: news of the clover roots
Swollen with April rains; of bugs and birds
Stirring with bright new life; of dandelions
Spreading their buttered crowns to the green and gold
Of soft spring showers—somehow they brought him news.

One morning a slim wan finger of the sun
That wriggled through the single grated window
High in the cellar, scrawled upon the floor
A slow gold syllable and fell aslant
A sack of parched green peas. A rill of peas
Dribbled from one torn corner, where mice,
Prowling at night, had gnawed the gunny-bag.
The stoic Waino held his empty eyes
An hour upon the peas; then, moved by a whim,
He rolled a keg of pickled fish, salt herring,
Into the sunlight and set it on an end.
He scraped his fingers on a barrel that held,
Thick on one broken hoop, a crust of mud
Scooped from the rain-soaked soil of the prison-yard
When it had fallen in loading; by patient clawing
He gathered handful on handful of the soil
And piled it on the floor. From a shattered box
He salvaged a scanty pound of fine-ground cork,
And from a bale a fistful of excelsior.
Puddling the whole with water in a pail,

He poured the synthetic earth upon the keg
Of pickled fish and formed a plot of soil
Bound by the jutting staves and a strip of tin
He lashed around the barrel-head to form a wall.

He gathered from the dribbling sack five peas;
Stabbing his thumb upon the dirt, he drew
The pattern of a cross, and solemnly
Into the form he poked his five parched peas,
Covered them firmly, and went about his work.

Each morning he drenched the rounded plot of earth
And scrutinized it eagerly for life.
One day he marked upon the black a cloud
Of thick soft green no larger than his palm.
He bent on it and knew the cloud of frail
Green spears at once as grass, a catch from beyond
The walls. He speculated on the passing bird
Whose bill had taken up the seeds, whose droppings
Had yielded him this gift of swelling life.
And when the blades of green were tall and thick
As fur on a gopher's back, he broke the clump
And patiently transplanted spear on spear
Over his barrel-garden to form a sod
Around his seeds.

         Another morning his eyes
Gleamed suddenly and wetly when they fell
On five white succulent stems that pierced the soil
And hungrily stretched for the wisp of passing sun.
Eagerly, day on day, he marked their growth:

The first faint lancing green that stabbed the soil,
The slow unfurling patch of velvet leaf,
The pea-vines eager to climb a little sky—
These glinted his eyes with the luster of a dream
And put in Waino's throat a quiet laughter
Like bubbles in the bottom of a well.

One Sunday morning Waino, loath to go
To hear the bellowing of the prison chaplain,
Sulked in his cellar and worshipped at his shrine
Of blossoming peas; bent on his barrel-plot,
He found delight in pruning the roving stems,
In sniffing at the new-blown crinkled petals,
And training the vines on tiny trellises.
The clatter of the cellar door, the creak
Of coming footsteps, brought him up alert.
He shambled out to meet a dim black figure
Groping among the bales—the half-breed, Fillion,
The bluffest voyageur on Lac la Croix,
Whose hot French blood had driven him to sink
A thirsty dagger to the fickle heart
Of Rose Labrie, the village courtesan;
His Indian strain of philosophic calm
And taciturnity had won for him
The freedom of a trusty.

                    "Those cook, La Plante,"
The Frenchman mumbled, "she's want one keg from herring.
M'sieu, you got one keg from fish in here?
Some place in cellar—yes?"

The eyes of Waino
Fluttered a moment; he drew his gnarled red hand
Dully across his forehead.

"No," he rasped,
"That fish—that keg of fish ain't here in warehouse."

"Bah Gar!" the Frenchman muttered, as the Finn
Shuffling, retreated to a dusky corner,
"Those cook M'sieu La Plante, she's got-it down
On inventory barrel from herring-fish
It's deliver-it last fall. I look around—
Me—I am look around; I find it—maybe."

Fumbling among the boxes, methodically
The mixed-blood penetrated every corner.
Furtively Waino stepped across the floor,
Planted his burly frame before the keg
To shelter it, and waited. Fillion came
At last and faced him, puzzled.

"Sacré! That's funny"—
Scratching his head—"those fish she ain't in here."

He turned to go, but as he wheeled, his eyes
Fell on a splash of green, a spray of leaves
That peeped around the elbow of the Finn.

"Ho-ho!" he laughed, "you got-it posies here?
She's pretty—yes?"

313

                    The white-faced Finn dropped back,
Trembling from crown to toe. The voyageur
Stepped forward to survey the patch of green
And sniff the blossoms.

                    "Mon Calvary!" he cried,
"That's keg from fish!—those keg she's growing on!"

Gorilla-like the Finn crouched sullenly
Beside the barrel and tensed the huge bunched hands
That dangled at his sides.

                    "That's fish all right
La Plante she's got-it on those inventory!
Almost I'm thinking—me—she's lost, those fish!"
Cried Fillion as he stooped to tilt the keg
And roll it to a truck.

                    The Finn crouched down;
Sharp fury flickered from his squinting eyes
Raggedly, hotly as the darting tongue
Of any badgered snake; his raw red throat
Rattled with stony syllables:

                    "Don't!—
Don't touch that fish! You take that keg, by Christ,
I break—I break your goddam back in two!"

Fillion glanced up an instant at the Finn,
Snorted, and wrapped his arms about the staves.
With a desperate roar the Finn flung up his head

And shattered the cold gray granite of his posture;
Lifting his groping hands above his head,
He clutched from on a shelf a syrup-jug
And crashed its huge black bulk on Fillion's skull.

The voyageur collapsed and sank to earth
Like an ox that drops beneath a butcher's sledge.
Minute on minute he sprawled upon the floor,
Stone-cold and stunned; a steaming crimson river
Spurted and dribbled from his severed scalp—
A ragged wound from his cow-lick to his ear.
Slowly his eyelids fluttered open; he gasped,
Rose to his knees and tottered to his feet—
Only to crumple like a hamstrung doe.
He struggled to his knees again and crawled
Blindly and dizzily across the floor
And up the steps to safety—while Waino huddled
Over his keg and shook with guttural sobs
That racked his ribs and rocked his huge broad back.

The warden, flanked by Clancy and Moran,
Came on him thus a dozen minutes later.
Hobbs fixed his cold gray eyes upon the Finn,
Slowly remarked his quivering shoulders, his head
Shaggy and wet with sweat, and driven deep
Into the vines upon the keg of fish.
Grimly he turned his interest to the plot—
The pulsing green of stem, the satin-white
Of petal, the rich cool pungence of the earth.
Slowly the iron of his jaw relaxed;
Gently and dubiously he wagged his head.

With something of a smile, a quizzical grin,
He muttered to Moran:

                  "Go tell La Plante
There is no keg of herring in the warehouse;
He must have been mistaken. And tell him, too,
To strike the item from the inventory."

Clancy, amazed, let down his lantern jaw
And stared; the warden was too much for him.

TWO WOODSMEN SKIN A GRIZZLY BEAR

How many thunderbolts, Brazzeau, were built
Into this beast? What iron strength reveals
Itself in every muscle!—as these wet knives
Strip off his rusty pelt and lay his carcass,
Bloody and steaming, open to the sun.

Those bear, M'sieu, she's biggest silvertip
That—me—I never seen. Mon Calvary!
She's weighing it a thousand pound—might be—
Those thundering brute.

                It's not a she, Bateese;
This monster is a he.

                Bedamme, don't tell me that!
Me—I am knowing it—she's plain enough;
Those grizzly she's a he.

                What slow sure power
Rippled along these bunched-up shoulder-blades,
When he went rambling through the hills; what strength
Rolled through his sliding flanks and down these muscles,
Gliding on one another, up and down
His length, like bands of lubricated steel.
When this wild creature was alive, Brazzeau,
Grim power rolled in him as in a sea,
Like combers breaking on an ocean beach.

Ocean? You're foolishness! She ain't no ocean—
Those bloody carcass; she's only silvertip!

Ocean! The writer-man she's coming out
From you, like rash or measles; you better let
Those ranger, she's also be in you—and hunter—
Do some your thinking. Ocean! She's only bear,
Dead bear, dead brute.

                        Maybe, and maybe not.
Somehow, there's something more in this warm body
Sprawled on the ground, so human in every curve—
So like a boy, a big fat naked boy,
Bateese, that every time I slip my knife
Into his flesh I also prick myself.
Something in this—oh, something troubles me,
Brazzeau; you skin him out and butcher him.
I'll rustle up the horses.

                        Mon Calvary!
You're getting soft. Ain't like you used to be.
She ain't no boy, no naked big fat boy;
She's bear, I'm telling you. That's plain to see
Like any horsefly in a glass of milk.
Bagosh, that gin we're drinking, she's touching you;
Only where others are seeing rattlesnakes
And elephant it's pink, you're seeing boys,
Bare-naked boys. That's only brute, damn brute,
A grizzly bear—I'm told you that.

                        I wonder!
I wonder if his mate, the groaning she
Who stumbled, whirled with terror when we shot,
And bolted up the draw to timber-line—

I wonder if to her this broken brute
Was only a grizzly—or a boy.

                              A grizzly,
Plain silvertip, of course.

                              Perhaps—perhaps.
But, listen! . . . Can't you hear her on the hog-back?
Bawling? . . . I wonder!

                                   Chut! Don't waste-it time
Wondering on her. Those he—might be you know it—
Was only killer anyway.

                    A killer?

Killer, for certainly! Those brute she's raid
The pig-pen from my neighbor, Archiquette,
And walk him off with two the fattest shoats
Under his arms—now ain't-it? That Kootenai Basin
It's better off without him.

                         Perhaps you're right.

Correct, my son! I'm right—ain't never wrong.
Come, come! Pick up those knife and help-it now.
We want those pelt—she's fetching twenty dollar,
Maybe, or more. It's coming dark and cold.
We got long way to ride before the night;
Ain't got no time to waste.

No doubt you're right;
No use in spending breath on any bear—
One more or less in the world . . . Now roll him over;
Spread out his legs. You skin one side of him;
I'll take the other. We'll strip him of his coat
As quickly as a seal can bolt a fish . . .
How stubborn to the blade—this hide! How tough! . . .
These thighs—as round as any red oak trunk—
These thighs have raised his body's bulk from earth
Ten thousand times, or more, as slowly, surely,
As any iron jack-knife bridge goes up
To let a creeping barge pass under it;
Straining his sinews, perhaps ten thousand times
They shoved his shoulders into cherry-boughs
Where he might gorge himself on dripping fruit.
Oh, there were hours in autumn when he reeled
Drunkenly through the bushes, slobbering
The fermented juice of frosted fruits, as drunk
And clownish as a lumberjack on pay day,
After a winter in the woods.

Those bear—
Grizzlies and blacks and browns, the all of them—
She's crazy for fruit, almost as much as bacon;
And funny when she's picking it the tree.
One day I see-it—me—a grizzly bear
Break him wild cherry sapling off the stump,
Stick him the broken tree upon his shoulder
Like maybe it's a flag or an umbrella,
And solemn march himself around a ring,
Like he don't know which way to go with it,

Or else he's on parade. That's funniest thing
That—me—I never seen!

                    One thing is droller:
A bear who's poked his paw inside a can
For left-over syrup, and trying clumsily
To bat it off; a can with jagged lips
Fastened upon a paw will always stump
A bear for hours and finally put the clown
To helter-skelter rout.

                    I see—me—that . . .
Bagosh, those flesh beneath the pelt she's warm,
And pink and clean like anything; those heart
Almost is beating; almost she seems alive . . .
Speaking from bears and fruits—the spoor from bear,
She's best damned calendar you never seen.
You're seeing-it those droppings in the woods
She's all pin-cherry stones, you know it's June,
Late in the month or early in July;
Chokecherry pits—that's later in July;
When spoor she's full those wild red raspberry seeds
She's middle summer; when she's color blue
From huckleberries, August is that month;
And blackberry seeds—she's coming on September.
Those calendar, bagosh, she's never fail—
Don't cost it nothing neither.

                    But why, Bateese—
Reckoning when the August sun has filled
Blueberries full of bursting purple juice—

Why search all day in a patch of huckleberries
To find blue spoor, to see if it is August?

Sacré de Dieu! Don't talk to me no more!
You're dumb like any bear.

                A bear's not dumb . . .
These forepaws, solid, stout, like iron clubs—
How often, do you think, Brazzeau, they locked
Themselves around a lazy mate in play
To wrestle him, or amiably cuffed
The hams of a grizzly cub to send it off,
Head over haunches, spinning like a pin-wheel
And squealing with delight? How often these paws
Clawed at the dirt for the roots of adders'-tongues,
Or ponderously plunged in clear cold brooks
To flip the pink and silver of a trout
Bouncing upon the bank?

                Ho-ho! my son, I see
Those grizzly fishing him those slippery trouts
Plenty the time; but—me—I never seen
Those slowpoke spear-it yet a crafty fish
And throw it on the bank. Sacré! he's clumsy;
Always he's plunging-it his paw too late—
After those trout she's run away and laugh
Upstream beneath a bank, a root, a rock.
That funny bear she's always sit him down
After and look and look, so puzzlement,
So sad, so foolish—he can't quite make it out.
God—or those Devil—don't intend that bears

Should ever catch-it trout she's in the brook;
But bears ain't knowing that! . . . Be careful now!—
Don't cut away so much the flesh and fat;
Later that makes it harder when we scrape
Those hide; go slower skinning—careful . . .

                                             Look!

Look here, Bateese! His left hind paw!

                                    His toes—
His toes ain't there! Bedamme, he's losing him
She's toes, the all of them!

                        A rusty trap,
Spitting and snarling as it crunched the bones,
Clamped down its jagged iron teeth on them.
Poor devil! I wonder what he made of it.
Did he, I wonder, bellowing with fear,
Drooling his rope of tongue, claw crazily
At the dogged jaws and spin with frenzy? How long
Do you suppose he studied the stubborn thing
And fumbled at the complicated steel
Before he surrendered? Did the badgered creature,
Blatting and bawling, drag the forty pounds
Of grinding metal two miles, or three, or four?
Did he, I wonder, beside himself with fright,
Furiously tear his paw from the grim red teeth
And limp off on his mangled stump of foot—
Leaving his toes—the price of liberty?
Or did he drag the vicious chain and log
Day upon day, until his gangrened toes

Dropped from their joints and he walked free again?
I wonder!

       Either way, the foot is heal
Again, almost as good like new—except
It ain't got toes.

       A toe, one more, one less,
Means little in the life of any grizzly
That struggles for survival.

       Or wolf or weasel . . .

Lift up his head, Brazzeau—a little more;
I'll run my knife around his skull—the eyes,
The ears, the nostrils. This part of our bloody job
Calls for a surer hand than mine. Now, steady! . . .
How often did this muzzle search the wind
For the taint of man-smell floating in the air?
How often did he rear and freeze with fright?

She's know-it that smell of man—correct—and plenty!
Those whole damned settlement is hunting him
Maybe a year or more.

       But you, Bateese,
You were the lucky devil!—smart enough
To bring him tumbling, groaning, down to earth.
Oh, what a shot, a perfect shot! . . . Look! Here!—
The base of the skull, this bunch of splintered bone—

Here, where your slug drilled daylight through his head—
A vital spot.

   Those spot, that base of brain,
She's deadlier than even shot in heart—
People ain't know that; but those place is small—
Ain't bigger than your fist; she's hard to hit,
When bear she's running.

     There was a trembling minute
When I was sure that we were checked for hell—
Clawed into ribbons, disemboweled. Remember?—
Your first wild shot that bit him in the shoulder,
And stung him like a wasp? How furiously
He whirled on us, unsteady on his legs,
Bellowing, batting madly at the air!
And when his mate went scrambling up to safety,
How quickly he wheeled from us, and, lashed by terror,
Pinned back his ears, and galloped for the peak!
Remember how he fell before your blast?
Crumpled to earth, like any oak-tree struck
By an avalanche, and crashed against the boulder?
Poor brute, I'll not forget how he dragged himself,
Blubbering, bleating, down the rocky slope
With heaving belly flat upon the ground;
Or how he writhed in the crimson pool that stained
The earth, and finally dropped his lathered jaws
Upon his outflung feet, and, with a sigh,
Sank gently to endless sleep—with never a bee,
A bug, a wolf to trouble him again.
Oh, what a kill! What a kill!

That was a good shot.
Me—I ain't trade my gun, my hand, my eye,
For any in the parish.

No doubt of that;
What with your eyes, Bateese, which look so straight—
Never around a corner, never slantwise—
What with your eyes, I'll venture you could kill
A humming-bird gone crazy with delight
In a honeysuckle bed, a butterfly
Dancing in May upon a windy meadow;
You wouldn't hesitate, I'll bet, to draw
A deadly bead upon that glorious star
Coming to life from out the night—Polaris.

Bedamme! And I—myself—could hit them, too—
Almost—except those North Star. But anyway,
Fooling you are; you're only making jokes.
Only damn' fool is shooting-it humming-birds
Or moths; that's only waste of lead and powder.
Butterflies, flowers, stars—they ain't no bear,
Or fox or coyote; they're only bugs and posies.
But grizzlies is grizzlies; something—something more
There is in grizzlies.

Granted! There is something,
A something more in galloping silvertips.
Grizzlies are grizzlies, that's plain enough, as clear
As the pebbles in the bottom of that brook.

And anyway, who wants to shoot-it stars!
You're only joking—maybe.

326

No doubt, Bateese.
Of course, a star is a million miles from us;
Rivière du Loup, and Henri Bisonette,
The trader in furs, are only twenty-one;
And the distance from your steady eyes and hands
Down to your belly is even less than that.
I haven't a leg to stand on.

Legs? Legs?
Whose talking from legs! or even bellies! Chut!
Excuse to me, my son, but did you fall
Maybe one time or another on your head
From out the arms your mother? when you was baby?
Bah! Legs!—you got-it plenty legs to stand on—
That's plain to see like nothing. Myself—I think
If anything you're lacking, might be brains—
They got-it cracks a little, a little wit-nit.
But I ain't going—me—to told you that;
Might be I make you feel-it very bad.

In any event, the valley is growing dark,
Black as the winter den of any bear.
We'd better ramble and make for the divide.
We'll get our bearings on "the Pass," the trail
To home, by star-glow; Polaris, yonder, will yield
What light—and truth and beauty—we may need
To travel these dark valleys of the world.
Squat on that mossy stone, and wait, Bateese—
And whistle up the stars. I'll wrangle the horses.

327

APPENDIX

APPENDIX

Most of the poems on Indian themes in Parts II, IV, VI, VII, IX, XI, and XII will yield their full meaning readily without the aid of supplementary comment on the Indian practices and beliefs involved in them. In nearly all these Indian studies I have incorporated within the poems themselves whatever special information on aboriginal customs, legends, and beliefs is pertinent to the poems. Moreover, I have made clear the correct pronunciation of the Chippewa words which occur in the poems by breaking the words into stressed and unstressed syllables and by spelling them exactly as they sound to the American ear. Further, I have incorporated the meanings of the Chippewa words in their immediate context.

A few of the poems, however, presuppose special knowledge of ceremonial practices, symbols, and beliefs which cannot be effectively incorporated in the poems themselves. In order to supply this information which is helpful in understanding these poems, and to further enrich their meaning, I submit this Appendix. I suggest that the reader glance at the supplementary comments on these special poems in Parts II, VI, IX, and XII before reading them.

PART II

THE BOX OF GOD

THE BOX OF GOD

Page 43

I am moved to speak at some length on "The Box of God," one of the more ambitious pieces in this collection. It would be helpful perhaps to discuss some of the red man's religious beliefs that lie at the foundation of this poem. There is much, no doubt, that could be said, and perhaps should be said, on this narrative, which not only records the conversion of a pagan Indian to Christianity in a mission among the forests north of Lake Superior, but also sets out aspects of the old, old struggle of all the human race, white as well as red, to find the Ultimate, to find God. Such a theme involves so many phases of Indian religion that one could throw light on some of the implications of the poem by discussing the spiritual outlook of the Indian as it is touched upon in this piece. But from another point of view further comment on this poem—beyond the definition of a few strange words—would be futile and inadequate. Some things one cannot say. I shall let the poem itself utter as best it can a portion of what I am moved to express at this moment.

The word "black-robes" for many years was the term used by Indians to indicate a Catholic priest and sometimes a Protestant missionary. The black-robed priests of the Roman Catholic Church were among the first missionaries to carry the gospel to the Indians of America. Undoubtedly they were among the most successful.

Contrary to popular belief, among the Indians the common name to designate a white man is not "pale face"—at any rate, not among the tribes I have known. The term used is "Big-Knife." The Chippewa (or Ojibway) Indians use the Chippewa word "Kéetch-ie Móh-ka-món" which means literally "Big Knife." It is obviously a reference to the sabers of the cavalrymen, of the Indian-fighters of the United States Army with whom the Indians of the West and the North came in early contact.

"K'tchée-gah-mee" is the Chippewa word for "Lake Superior." It means literally "Big-Water" or "Big-Lake." It is a corruption of the correct word, "Kéetch-ie Gáh-mee," or "Géetch-ie Gáh-mee" (the consonants "k" and "g"—also "b" and "p" and "d" and "t"—are interchangeable in the Chippewa language—different bands of Ojibways sound them differently). But "K'tchée-gah-mee," the colloquial corruption of the formally correct word, is the word actually used by the red inhabitants of the forests north of Lake Superior.

"Kéetch-ie Má-ni-dó," the central theme of this poem, means "Big Spirit." In the religion of the Chippewa the universe is peopled with many "má-ni-dós," with many spirits or gods. Some of them reside in eagles and bears, others in the four winds, in the sun, in thunder, and there are many other minor spirits. But high above them all, in supreme command, is "Kéetch-ie Má-ni-dó"—the Great Mystery.

The word "Shing-ób" means "spruce." It is the surname of the central character in the narrative—Joe Shing-ób, or Joe Spruce.

"Ah-déek," which means "caribou," is the Indian name given to Joe Spruce's white friend and companion.

"Chée-sah-kée" refers to the "black-medicine-men" who

333

conjure the aid of evil spirits rather than that of good spirits.

The pidgin-English utterances of Joe Spruce in "II: Whistling Wings" are obviously a strange blending of Indian idiom and French-Canadian patois. The origin of this common dialect of the northern Indian may be readily understood when one recalls that the French explorers, fur-traders, and voyageurs long before our nation was established found their way to the wilderness of the Lake Superior region—to what is now Minnesota, Michigan, Wisconsin, and Ontario. Many of the Frenchmen remained among the Chippewas and married into the tribe. As a result, Chippewas have more than a dash of French blood. Many words in the Chippewa language are corruptions of original French words. Consequently, the pidgin-English dialect of the Indian reveals much French influence.

PART VI
FLYING MOCCASINS

THE SQUAW-DANCE

Page 117

The songs and dances of the American Indian are almost beyond calculation. Assuredly the complete range and number of them are not known to any white man, or even to any Indian. First, consider the fact that there are many Indian nations and each nation embraces many tribes. These nations and tribes differ somewhat—often much—in their beliefs and practices, in their religion, their music, and their dances. They all have songs and dances peculiarly their own. Furthermore, a single tribe—for example, the Chippewas who dwell chiefly in Minnesota, Wisconsin, Michigan, and Canada—may possess a vast variety of songs and dances: the music and ceremonies of the many medicine-societies; "dream" songs and love songs; "give-away" dances, begging dances, pipe dances, and war-dances; songs for gambling games, for the presentation of gifts, for funerals and mourning; songs for the entertainment of children, for periods of fasting, for curing the sick, for celebrating good harvests, for insuring good crops, good fishing, good hunting—oh, there are many more. But not only every tribe has its vast number of songs and dances but also every individual medicine-man and singer knows and uses songs peculiarly his own. They are his private property, for they came to him in a dream induced by fasting and they involve his private "spirit-helper," the spirit of the particular bear or tree or buffalo who came to him in his dream. No man knows, and no man will

335

ever know, all the songs, dances, and ceremonies of the Indians of America.

In all his music-making the Indian uses only a few instruments: a variety of drums—water-drums, tom-toms, and a huge drum on which several Indians beat simultaneously in the center of the dancing-ring; bells of many kinds, chiefly sleigh-bells, rattles, gourds with pebbles in them or dried substances; and occasionally he uses whistles of hollow bone. In his love songs and serenades the northern woods Indian uses the Bée-bee-gwún, a cedar flute on which he usually plays a simple but wistful tune.

Although there is great variety in the songs and dances of the American Indian, one type of dance is well-nigh universal. It is called the "Squaw-Dance," the "Woman's Dance," or most often perhaps, the "Give-away Dance." Nearly every tribe has preserved some variation of this social dance. But all the variations are basically alike in rhythm, ideas, and spirit. It is a "good-time" dance in which both men and women participate. It is one of the few dances in which women may participate. This is the ceremony upon which the poem "The Squaw-Dance" is built.

"The Woman's Dance" is often held on the Fourth of July, or to celebrate the end of a period of mourning, or for exhibition purposes before white tourists, or at any other time when the band is disposed to have a "good-time dance."

In this performance most of the men and women arrange themselves in a big circle around the group of men beating a big ceremonial drum in the center of the ring. The Indians in the circle shuffle to the left steadily and rhythmically to the beat of the drummers and their lively singing. Within the circle, at the center of the ring, individual men dance robustly. There is occasional laughter, and always there is happiness in this dance. But Indians as a rule tend to be somewhat sober and earnest of countenance when they are enjoying themselves profoundly. As someone has said, they take their fun seriously.

It is customary in this ceremony for some of the Indians dancing in the center of the ring to select a friend in the shuffling circle—or an onlooker—and present a gift to him, a plug of tobacco, a pair of moccasins, a buckskin shirt—I have seen Indians give away their favorite ponies and eagle-bonnets with scores of plumes valued at one dollar a plume. Whereupon the recipient of the gift must dance in the center of the ring with the friend thus complimenting him, and later he must return the honor with a gift of equal value. And thus, with occasional interruptions for the giving away of presents, all day and all night the celebration continues vigorously.

This poem, "The Squaw-Dance," is written from the point of view of an *onlooker*—not of a participant in the dance. I have tried to capture the meaning of the dance, its procedure, and its spirit in order to give the reader a good grasp of what an Indian dance looks like, sounds like, and means. In addition I have preserved accurately the basic rhythm of the "Squaw-Dance" which is characteristic of many other Indian dances. I urge the reader to grasp the rhythm in the poem because it is clearly expressed and easily felt in this piece, and because if he establishes in his ear the rhythm of this poem, he has the key to the basic Indian rhythms in most aboriginal dances.

In reading this dance-poem aloud, the reader should establish and maintain steadily the vigorous beat of an Indian

337

drum which is built into the cadence of the lines. He should depart from this robust drum-rhythm only in the solo-speeches by "Kee-wáy-din-ó-kway" and "Mah-éen-gans" when they bestow their gifts.

THE BLUE DUCK

Page 122

We said a moment ago that Indian songs and dances are infinite in number—as numerous as grass. Even a single category of Indian music may be beyond classifying. This is especially true of medicine-songs and medicine-dances.

It is difficult to define the word "medicine" as it is used by Indians. It does not necessarily mean ointments and medicines to cure the sick. It is a larger, more inclusive term than this. Some aspects of medicine-making bear upon religion, or mystical supernatural experience. Other aspects involve conjuring, magic, spiritism. And still others involve the use of herbs, objects, and substances which have therapeutic properties in the mind of the Indian. At any rate, the old-time Indian turned to the medicine-man for aid in almost every aspect of life and of living. The medicine-man was at once a priest, a physician, and a conjurer.

The number of medicine-songs and ceremonies is beyond calculation. Every medicine-man possesses not only the common property of songs and rituals given to him as a member of the medicine-society, but he also possesses his own special, potent "medicines," which no other medicine-man may know. As a consequence, there are many kinds of "medicine": medicine to make a good hunting season for the Indian who wishes to trap beavers, minks, martens, fishers;

338

medicines for curing the lame, the blind, the tuberculous; medicines to bring a curse down on an enemy; medicines to win the love of another; medicines that make for success in war; medicines for mourners and widows; medicines for those who may for any reason wish to commune with the dead; medicines for the period of puberty when boys retire into a remote forest and go into a period of fasting in order to "dream" and in the dream discover their "spirit-helper"; "owl medicine," "rain medicine," and "fire-charm medicine"; and many others, as many as the individual medicineman in his imagination may create in order to supply the demand of his clients.

"The Blue Duck" is a free interpretation of a hunting medicine-song. It is based on the medicine-making of John Still-Day, at one time the ablest medicine-man on the Red Lake Indian Reservation in Minnesota. Still-Day was regarded as especially effective in making hunting and trapping medicine.

In some medicine rituals it is customary for the medicineman to carve out of cedar a small image of the person, the animal, or the object which is the central figure in the ceremony or the situation. Thus, for example, in the making of love medicine the conjurer always carves a small image of the person of the opposite sex whom one wishes to captivate, and the image is used in the ritual. In the hunting medicine involved in "The Blue Duck" the medicine-man carves an image of a duck—the central figure in his conjuring; the figure is a symbol about which much of the ritual revolves.

In the medicine-song the medicine-man invokes Kéetch-ie Má-ni-dó, "The Big Spirit," to send down from the North a

339

big flight of ducks for the fall hunt and in general to make a season of good hunting and trapping.

"Kéetch-ie Má-ni-dó," a name which appears frequently in the Indian poems in this book, means literally, "Big Spirit," and, broadly, "The Great Mystery," "God." In the mind of the Chippewa of pagan faith, the world is peopled with many "má-ni-dós," or spirits. These spirits are good and evil. One of the most powerful of them lives in the bear— the Mák-wa Má-ni-dó. A very good spirit lives in the green frog. An old pagan Indian will never hurt a green frog; he will look at you aghast if you fasten one on a barbed hook as bait for a bass. One of the most evil má-ni-dós lives in the little red frog who makes his home in the rotten stumps of trees. Another evil spirit is "Mú-chie Má-ni-dó"; he resembles somewhat the white man's devil. There are five spirits stronger than these, however; four of them are the spirits who live in the points of the compass and in the four winds, North, East, South, and West; the fifth is the god called "Thunderbird." These five great spirits, however, are merely lieutenants of "The Big Spirit." Above all these minor deities rules "Kéetch-ie Má-ni-dó."

In the oral rendition of "The Blue Duck," the reader should establish a robust up-and-down drum-beat rhythm in the first few lines and adhere to it steadily, except when the poem rises to the level of a chant, or a wail, or a prayer.

THUNDERDRUMS

Page 127

This poem is a free interpretation of a war-medicine ceremony performed often in the old days of the Chippewas as

340

a part of their preparations for war with the Sioux, their bitter enemies. The ancient war-dance has been preserved by some of the tribes and is performed occasionally by the Red Lake Chippewas.

A brief description of a war-dance and a study of the poem, "Thunderdrums," will reveal the futility of translation as a method of capturing the ideas and the spirit of Indian songs and dances.

In the war-dance while the chiefs and the braves danced in the ring for long periods and worked themselves into a high emotional pitch in preparation for a battle, the medicine-men made war-medicine. By means of their chants and their "good medicines" they would render the warriors immune from injury and death; they would invoke the aid of the powerful spirits, especially the spirit of the Thunderbird. They would endow the tribal warriors with uncommon powers, and thus strengthen the fighting hearts of the braves. The ceremony might continue for hours, yet in the entire period few specific words would be uttered, beyond an exultant *"Ah-hah-háy!"* or *"Háh-yah-ah-háy!"* or a defiant war-whoop, or a blood-curdling shout. Yet consider all that occurred: long periods of dancing, of dramatic posturing, and pantomime, of singing and drumming which varied from time to time in idea and spirit; periods of meaningful medicine-making and invocations. A literal translation of the few words uttered in this dance would reveal little.

But this is not all. In the course of the dance individual braves would perform solo dances. By means of gesture, posture, and pantomime one Indian would enact a dramatic scene; he would tell the story of a former battle in which he had killed an enemy in a hand-to-hand struggle. Another

341

Indian would portray in his dance-pantomime how he planned to trail, attack, and destroy his foes. A third might impersonate animals or men and horses wounded in battle, or he might enact a score of dramatic incidents relevant to the war-medicine dance. In "Thunderdrums," Sections II-V, "Double-Bear Dances," "Big-Sky Dances," "Ghost-Wolf Dances," and "Iron-Wind Dances," I have sought to capture the spirit of four solo dances or pantomimes typical of many others in the old war-medicine ceremonies.

The dance-pantomime is the root of Indian drama. It is the only form of drama known to the early American Indians, with the exception of certain seasonal dances and ambitious religious ceremonies—and most of these ceremonies are simply elaborations of the more common dance-pantomimes.

The Thunderbird, mentioned often in this poem, is easily one of the most powerful of all the spirits in the supernatural world of the red man. He plays an important role in the conjuring of medicine-men. The Thunderbird comes to the world in electric storms; he manifests himself when the black clouds gather on the horizon, when the sky rumbles with thunder, and the flaming bolts and jagged lightnings flash overhead.

The word "Cut-throat" is the term used by Chippewas occasionally to characterize the Sioux Indian. The word "Pucker-skin" is sometimes used by the Sioux to describe the Chippewa. Chippewa moccasins were fashioned out of buckskin with seams that puckered peculiarly. Hence the name.

The expressions *Ho! Hó!*, *Ah-hah-háy!*, *Háh-yah-ah-háy!*, and *Wuh!* are typical Chippewa explosives and ejaculations of approval and enthusiasm by the audience. The war-medicine dance is peppered with them from the first beat of the drum to the last. Since they represent high peaks of emotion, moments when one cannot find words to express one's feelings, these grunts and shouts are usually blood-stirring in a real war-dance.

The rhythm of the poem is peculiarly Indian; it is the drum-beat rhythm most basic and common among the Chippewa Indians. In the oral rendition of the poem it is imperative that the reader establish at once this vigorous up-and-down drum-beat rhythm and maintain it steadily and robustly throughout the piece. If the reader grasps and renders the vigorous and persistent drum-beat cadence of this poem, he will have the rhythmic key to most of the Indian dance-poems in this book.

INDIAN LOVE SONG

Page 132

The love songs of the Indian and the love serenades played on the cedar flute are as a rule plaintive in spirit. "Indian Love Song" is typical of the spirit of most Indian love songs and it suggests their characteristic ideas.

INDIAN SLEEP SONG

Page 133

In the lodges of the more remote Indians one may still see Indian cradle-boards and hear old Indian lullabies. The "tík-in-áh-gun," or cradle-board, is made of basswood on which the Indian baby is bound with beaded cloth and buckskin. This board serves as a cradle and a carrying-board. When a mother wishes her baby to fall asleep, she improvises a hammock from blankets swung between two lodge-poles, places in it the cradle-board to which the baby is lashed, and she sings while she swings the hammock to and fro.

The lullabies of the Indian mother are in spirit much like those of the white mother, except that perhaps they are more plaintive and they usually contain few words—other than the syllables "Wáy-way-wáy" or "Wé-we-wé" or some variation of these. In "Indian Sleep Song" I have endeavored to capture the spirit of a typical Indian lullaby, and the rhythm of a swinging cradle-board.

CRAZY-MEDICINE

Page 135

One of the medicines in demand among Indians, even today, is "revenge medicine." If an Indian seeks revenge against an enemy or a hated rival, he will probably go to a medicine-man who may select an incantation known as "crazy-medicine." In making "crazy-medicine," the conjurer carves a small cedar image of the foe of his client as large as a man's finger, and on a string he suspends it from an arched willow switch, so that the image may toss and spin freely in the wind. Touching its head with vermilion medicine-paint, he addresses the image as if it were his client's enemy in the flesh. The poem, "Crazy-Medicine," expresses the ideas behind the symbol, behind the conjuring, and in the mind of the medicine-man.

Page 136

Most Indian love songs express the spirit of loneliness, wistfulness, and melancholy. Sometimes they are somewhat romantic and idealistic in their form of utterance. The circumstances which usually attend the singing of love songs and the playing of serenades on the Bée-bee-gwun make for a romantic setting; the young buck often slides out into the lake in a birch-bark canoe at dusk, or on a moonlight night, and he plays his cedar flute for some young woman back in the village. The picture is pretty. But behind the idealized picture the spirit of love in the heart of the young man is very old, very real, and somewhat elemental.

The poem, "Beat Against Me No Longer," does not reflect the most common type of idealized Indian love song, or the spirit of the melancholy romanticized cedar flute theme, or the ideas most typical of love songs—"I am lonely— thinking about you—weeping for you"; but it does capture the love song in the heart of the Indian, the more realistic spirit that governs the hearts of most Indians in their love making.

The lines beginning, "Be not as the flat-breasted squaw-sich . . . who hides three sleeps in the forest," refers to an Indian custom that requires a girl approaching adolescence, manifesting the first signs of coming womanhood, to leave the village and live alone in a wigwam in the woods for a period.

Page 138

Some chants are personal and private, not tribal or communal. Many Indians possess "medicine" of their own and private "spirit-helpers"; they do not depend on medicine-men. "Chant for the Moon-of-Freezing" is a personal prayer. It is typical of hundreds of others in the general nature of its ideas, in its spirit, and in its paradoxes.

RED-ROCK, THE MOOSE-HUNTER

Page 140

When the primitive Indian of the Canadian North went hunting in the old days, he "called" or lured moose by two methods. Sometimes with a folded piece of birch-bark at his lips he would imitate the blare and bellow of a moose. This mode of "calling" still survives among woods Indians in moose-country and is often used by white men. There was another method, however, not well-known to white men. At dusk, when the wind went down and the water was quiet, when it is the habit of moose to come out of the "bush" to the lakes, to drink, to feed upon the lily-roots, and to plunge into the water in order to shake off the moose-flies, the deer-flies and the "no-see-ums"—then the Indian would wade into the water of any quiet lake used much by moose—they have their favorite watering places. Here for hours the Indian would imitate the splashings and drippings of a feeding moose, on the theory that moose in the neighborhood in the tranquil evening would hear the sounds and would be drawn to the immediate vicinity of the hunting

Indian. "Red-Rock, the Moose-Hunter," is based on this old, uncommon technique of "calling" moose.

TO A DEAD PEMBINA WARRIOR

Page 142

Among many of the woods Indians of the North, tree-burial was a common practice. When an Indian died in the winter, in the time of ice, deep snow, and bitter cold, it was the custom to dispose of the body by placing it in a tree until spring when the ground thawed sufficiently for the digging of a grave. The body was placed in a tree in order to keep it out of the reach of coyotes and timber-wolves. In the tree-burial practice, the dead Indian was wrapped about with an inner layer of blankets and an outer layer of birch-bark which was stitched with fibers of roots or buckskin and sealed with pitch; the birch-bark coffin was then placed in a scaffold in the crotch of a tree.

"To a Dead Pembina Warrior" is not an Indian song. It is an original poem addressed to an Indian chief who was killed by his enemies in hostile territory and was given a tree-burial.

SCALP-DANCE

Page 144

In the old days of the Indian wars, the prized possessions of Indian braves were the scalps which they had taken in battle from the heads of their enemies. The scalps actually captured in the lifetime of the average warrior were few—not nearly so many as popular belief would suggest. But the few were precious to the possessor. They were moving symbols to him, symbols of his bravery and his prowess. They played an important role frequently in his dancing, especially in his war-dances and his war-medicine songs. The poem, "Scalp-Dance," records not only the elemental rhythm of a war-medicine dance, but also the freight of ideas suggested by the symbols and by the dancing.

THE WINDS OF FIFTY WINTERS

Page 189

The council-oratory of the Indian is interesting in its range and variety. Naturally the beauty and power of any council-talk depends largely on the character of the speaker, on his imagination, on his intelligence, and on other personal traits. Some Indian orators are most effective; others are dull—they drool and drawl in their speaking, exactly as some white speakers do. But on the whole Indian council-speaking offers a fascinating study. Those things peculiarly Indian in the red man shine out most clearly in his council-speaking: his simplicity; his talent for irony; his vivid imagery; his basic dignity; his earthiness; and his genuine power.

In order to provide a scenic background for this group of council-talks, I wish to describe a typical council. A council is a more or less official gathering of Indians for the purpose of determining matters of tribal concern and of formulating tribal policies. It is a place for debating and discussing tribal legislation. It is a thoroughly democratic institution—except that it is usually dominated by the chiefs and the old men whose wisdom and mandates are invariably respected by the tribe. In the old days councils were called often between different tribes in order to settle their differences or for friendly visitations. Sometimes they were held between Indians and white men—usually officers in the United States Army—in order to make treaties.

In recent years, however, the most important councils are

349

called to iron out tribal difficulties with our government. Although the Indians of today are citizens of the United States, most of them are wards of our federal government. Their affairs are supervised and administered in part by the United States Department of the Interior through the Office of Indian Affairs. Whenever this agency of the government wishes to investigate tribal conditions, complaints, or problems or to confer with Indians on the formulation of new tribal policies, a council is called. The Indians in attendance may number a few dozen or several hundred. At this meeting spokesmen for the Indians—usually chiefs and headmen —state their cases through official interpreters to the representative of the Department of the Interior. A court reporter records the speeches as they are interpreted and later they are filed in Washington.

The councils are usually marked by dignity, orderliness, and seriousness. The audience is usually attentive and respectful. It is on the whole undemonstrative except for an occasional expression of approval. In most of the council-poems I have indicated the typical Chippewa exclamations of approval and linguistic applause by inserting them in the poems.

"The Winds of Fifty Winters" is a poetic version of a famous Chippewa council-talk which is spoken of as a classic among old Chippewa Indians. It is recalled always with a chuckle.

MEDALS AND HOLES

Page 193

For many reasons this poem and most of the other council-talks were written in the broken pidgin-English which a not too civilized and pretentious mixed-blood interpreter at a council would use, rather than in the linguistically elegant language of the white man's formal oratory. Too often official interpreters who have translated addresses made in government councils, historians who have recorded famous Indian orations, and novelists and playwrights who have sought to capture Indian speech, have lost much of the flavor of genuine Indian oratory. In their desire to intensify the romantic element or to make the speech of the Indian more easily comprehended by the white man often they have fallen back on the formal rhetoric of the white man. As a result, our recorded Indian speeches are sometimes too formal, too studied, too elegant and heroic. The few examples of Indian oratory available in the English language are sometimes more white man than Indian in spirit. The genuine beauty of his speech, its simplicity and naïveté, its broad and subtle humor, its moments of grandeur, its earthiness and brute power— these have been too often smothered and lost in rhetorical elegance and ornamentation.

Moved, therefore, by a desire to preserve the less romantic but perhaps more vital aspects of his speech, I offer this council-talk and most of the other council-talks with the hope that their loss in fluency and polish which results from the broken dialect in which they are written may be offset by their gain in spontaneity and naturalness, in ruggedness and sense of reality, and in the beauty of stark truth.

The frequent references to "the golden medal" go back to the days when the Kéetch-ie Ó-gi-má, the "Big Chief" of the white man, the President of the United States, seeking to win the friendship and the support of influential chiefs, often awarded them big medals. Indians are usually naive in their love of honors and ornaments. Therefore they prized the medals presented them by the government; the medals were big, gleaming, impressive.

Usually most of the speaking in council is done by the chiefs and the old men. Some of the speakers are very old, querulous, and on the verge of second childhood. The speaker in this poem is typical of some of the very old men who speak often, at great length, and sometimes on the most trivial matters.

CHIEF BEAR'S-HEART "MAKES TALK"

Page 195

I include this poem because it is typical of dozens of council-talks I have heard. Moreover, the problems raised in it and the conditions mentioned were at one time—not so long ago—well-nigh universal; they were common not only among the Chippewas but also the Sioux, the Potawatomies, the Winnebagos and many other tribes. They are still fairly typical and common but they are much less acute. Since 1932 the federal government, through an uncommonly strong Department of the Interior and an effective Office of Indian Affairs, has instituted far-reaching reforms and as a consequence the condition of the Indian has been improved immeasurably.

Most of the remaining poems in this group are poetic council-talk interpretations suggested by speeches actually made at many councils held by the government and Chippewa Indians for the discussion of certain violations of the "Treaty of 1854," the "Treaty of 1889" and other agreements. Many of the grievances expressed in these monologues obviously represent but one point of view, the Indian's version of the dispute. Often they may be traced to misunderstanding, or to the misinterpretation of a document, or to Indian prejudice and unreasonableness, or to some characteristic Indian weakness. Even so, there is usually in the Indian's cause a good measure of truth and some adequate ground for complaint. The government has not always been as understanding, as intelligent, and as efficient in administering Indian affairs as it is today. The white men who have done business with the Indian have not always been above cunning, chicanery, and exploitation. There was a time, moreover, when Indians were more gullible and less wise in the artifices of the white man than they are today.

Recording the poetry in the council-oratory of the Indians presents a problem. If one tries to capture the rugged beauty of Indian speech in the flawless diction and the well-turned sentences of the white man, one may gain in the clearness and coherence of one's writings. But he gains them at a price; the writings tend to lose the flavor of genuine Indian speech with its limited vocabulary of strong nouns and verbs, its crudities and distortions, and its rich idiom. Therefore, in order to preserve at any cost the Indian elements in his language and the genuine poetry of his utterances, I have chosen to write most of the council-talks in this book in the dialect spoken by some of the older—and more typical—Indians of the North, on the theory that this pidgin-English of the remote Indian registers more accurately than the white man's smooth rhetoric the earthy poetry in Indian speech.

The phrases "Boo-zhóo"! and "Boo-zhóo nee-chée"! are forms of the friendly salutation common among the Chippewas. Obviously they are corruptions of the French "Bonjour"! of Canadian-French voyageurs and coureurs des bois.

LITTLE-CARIBOU "MAKES BIG TALK"

Page 200

This poem is based on a council-talk I heard about 1910 at Cass Lake, Minnesota. It is an interpretation of the talk given by a weazened old man. His speech was typically Indian in its humor, in its wryness, and in its spirit in general.

Many white folk believe that the Indian lacks a sense of humor; that he never laughs or jokes; that he is always the taciturn and sullen red man of the theatre, the circus, the cinema. Many believe, too, that all the ideas he possesses and all the emotions he experiences may be expressed in one word: "Ugh"! How amusing!—and false! True, in formal meetings and in his dealings with the white man the Indian is usually a man of few words, and he is solemn and reserved. But among his own people and in the circle of his family he laughs often and much. Moreover, the women and children seem to be forever laughing, joking, and giggling over nothing. Among the older folk in every Indian tribe are many droll characters, men who possess at once Indian dignity and reserve and a rare sense of humor. The poem, "Little-Caribou 'Makes Big Talk'" deals with this little known side of the Indian.

In council-meetings and elsewhere as a rule the red man is deferential and courteous to elderly people. In this poem, therefore, the jibes and interruptions by the young Indians and the "asides" and the colloquy between Little-Caribou and his young hecklers (represented by the indented stanzas in italics) are unusual.

FIRE-BENDER TALKS
Page 203

Game wardens and Indians have carried on a running fight for many decades. There is always a hot issue between reservation Indians and conservation officers. Most red men do not hesitate to violate the game laws of a state; some hunt and fish in season and out of season—whenever they wish food. Behind this obstinate, persistent violation of the game-laws is an interesting point of view, a way of thinking, which I have embedded in this council-talk.

WHIRLING-RAPIDS TALKS
Page 206

The allegory, "Whirling-Rapids Talks," illustrates the tendency of the Indian to symbolize human experience. The habit of personifying nature, of attributing personality to every bird that soars and to every beast that walks or crawls on earth, and of symbolizing all life by the sun and the moon, by water and thunder and lightning—this is the essence of his imagination. Because of these habits of interpreting nature and because of his profound understanding of the wild earth and his close contact with every aspect of wild life, it is safe to say that no race has ever established a more intimate or moving communion with nature than has the American Indian.

PART XII

RED GODS

WEENG

Page 265

Like white folk, Indians have trouble persuading their children to go to sleep at night. But the Chippewa Indian has an advantage over the white man; he has the assistance of a god who has charge of children and of sleep. His name is "Wéeng-oosh" or "Weeng." He is a spirit no larger than one's thumb. Even in this modern day, in many Indian homes in the north woods at night one may see an old grandmother take over a child who is fighting slumber and put him to sleep with a story or a song about "Wéeng-oosh." The poem "Weeng" is a slumber-song based upon the legend of old "Sleepy-eye," "Wéeng-oosh."

In the oral rendition of this poem the reader should chant the lines quietly and monotonously with the slow sing-song rhythm that marks most of the lullabies of the white man and of the Indian.

THE BIRTH OF WÁY-NAH-BO-ZHÓO

Page 267

Wáy-nah-bo-zhóo is an important legendary character among the Chippewa Indians. The prowess of this strange, inconsistent hero is set out in scores of folk-tales. He emerges from these many myths a self-contradictory, unbelievable half-god: he is at once angelically good and devilishly bad; he is gentle and he is cruel; he is guileless and he is cunning.

An explanation for his caprices and his inconsistencies may be found in this broad interpretation of the legend of the birth of Wáy-nah-bo-zhóo.

The short, indented stanzas which record the "asides" of the narrator of the legend suggest an interesting aspect of some Indians: the sharp contrast between the beauty and power of the Indian in his official character as a medicine-man, an orator, or a teller of folk-tales and the earthy reality of the Indian as a simple human being. In the latter character the red man often has a salty savor and a pungence, like broiled venison.

CHANT FOR THE MOON-OF-FLOWERS

Page 276

Many prayers, chants, and songs of the woods Indians involve as part of their ritual tossing on the fire a bit of kinnikinic, an Indian tobacco made of red willow bark. The ascending smoke goes up to the Big Spirit and carries the prayer of the Indian. This common ritual lies at the base of this chant for good crops.

MAPLE-SUGAR CHANT

Page 278

The Indian is vitally dependent upon nature. His economic life and his social life revolve about nature. His spiritual life is built entirely upon nature in its manifold forms and moods. In his personal life from day to day, he is in constant communion with nature. Whenever an old pagan Indian goes hunting and kills a bear, he may offer up a prayer to the spirit who is known as Chief-of-the-Bears. He explains the necessity that drove him to kill one of the Bear-Chief's subjects, he expresses his sorrow, and he thanks him for permission to take one of his children. If the sky is ominous with black thunder-clouds and jagged lightning and the pine-trees bend and groan before the wind, the Thunderbird-spirit is coming; in this situation the devout Indian of the old days would toss a pinch of tobacco on the fire as a peace-offering to the Thunderbird and would make a short prayer to placate him. If the special spirit-helper of an Indian lives in the Norway pine-trees, Norway pines are "good medicine"; and whenever he encounters an especially tall and lovely Norway pine, he will stop and commune with it for a minute.

"Maple-Sugar Chant" is based on a seasonal ceremony that illustrates the spiritual significance of most Indian ceremonies and the depth of reality of the Indian's feeling for everything in, on, and of the earth.

When the first warm days and frosty nights of early spring arrive, Indians pack their kettles, buckets, and household goods and move to the sugar-bush. There they build their lodges and prepare to make their annual supply of maple-sugar. Before they embark on the business of making sugar, however, a feast must be given to Mother Earth, and to Wáy-nah-bo-zhóo, the legendary character regarded by Chippewas as a powerful guardian spirit. Several old women must first gather a few buckets of the early run of maple-sap. They must avoid touching or tasting the sap. When the fluid has been boiled down, the sugar is set aside for the ceremony to be held later in the day. In the evening, around the huge fire, a feast is spread for all the families in the camp. One place is left vacant; a platter of the sugar especially prepared by the old women is set at that place for Wáy-nah-bo-zhóo whose spirit will come out of the night during the ceremony, to join in the feast, to eat the maple-sugar prepared for him, and to bless the tribe with a good sugar season, with a great run of rich and plentiful sap. "Maple-Sugar Chant" is not a description of the ceremony; it is an interpretation of the spiritual meanings of this seasonal feast.

SPOTTED-FACE, THE TRIBAL FOOL, PRAYS

Page 282

Often Indian chants, ceremonies, and council-talks contain a strange blending of the idealistic and the realistic, of the sublime and the crass. This chant illustrates the fairly common practice of combining these incongruous elements.

FEAST FOR THE MOON-OF-BREAKING-SNOWSHOES

Page 284

Seasonal chants and ceremonies are common among all Indian tribes. Parts I and II of this poem suggest the nature of a seasonal chant and the high level of utterance and the dignity which Indian ceremonies at their best achieve. I added Part III, in which "Hands-over-the-Sun" speaks to individuals in the group and urges them to pay adequately for the services rendered them by the medicine-men, in order to suggest the materialism that may also mark Indian ceremonies.

The word "medicine" is a broad, ambiguous word in the Indian language. It may mean anything from "herbs" to "conjuring," from "magic," to "religion." There are many kinds of medicine and several types of medicine-man. One type which is rapidly disappearing is the "chée-sah-kée," the conjurer, the medicine-man who is in league with bad spirits rather than with good spirit-helpers. He is in a sense a conjurer and a spiritualist. He performs several remarkable feats of magic.

His chief performance, however, is that of conjuring the spirits of the dead into his wéeg-i-wam, or "chée-sah-kán." Several Indians with personal problems that require the help of "the spirits," or who for any of a dozen reasons wish to speak with the dead, may ask the "chée-sah-kée" to "make medicine" for them.

At a designated time the Indians go to the woods with the "chée-sah-kée," and he builds a wéeg-i-wam of birch-bark and stout lodge-poles which are planted so firmly in the earth that they cannot be moved easily by a human being. The "chée-sah-kée" builds a fire before the lodge, squats before the flame, beats his drum and begins to chant. Soon or late the lodge begins to sway gently from right to left. It increases steadily in the vigor of its movements until bells tied to the peak of the lodge-poles begin to jingle. These signs indicate that "the spirits" are within the chée-sah-kán, or lodge, and are ready to communicate with anybody in the circle of Indians who may pose problems and ask questions. The onlookers who had asked the medicine-man to "make chée-sah-kán" and to produce the spirits talk one by one with their favorite spirits—the spirit of a dead relative, or of an animal "má-ni-dó."

If a conjurer ever fails to set the lodge to dancing and to fill the lodge with spirits ready to talk, it is not the fault of his religion or medicine; it means simply that a rival of his is defeating him or some jealous spirit is working against him.

My old Indian friend, Áh-zhay-waince, "Other-Side," a medicine-man of the Pigeon River Reservation, used to perform this feat. I saw him cause his lodge to rock violently with spirits one night in the deep woods of the Canadian border north of Lake Superior, and I heard the voices of the spirits of dead Indians, of an otter, a beaver and a bear speak from within the lodge. They all spoke the Chippewa language. The many voices were marked by the same vocal timbre. All the speakers had the same dialectic eccentricities and inflections. Obviously the performance was a clever piece of conjuring, a baffling trick that involved an accomplice. But to most old-time Indians it is no trick; it is "good medicine."

"The Conjurer" is a free interpretation of the chant of the Chée-sah-kée and of the performance. The short, indented lines and stanzas in the poem are the conjurer's "asides" to his Indian audience.

RAIN SONG

Page 291

This interpretation of a medicine-song for making rain is based on an old Indian superstition. During the medicine ritual a buckskin sack containing small mica-like scales is

361

placed on a boulder by a stream near the scene of the ceremony. These bits of mica—"rain medicine"—are believed to be scales from the body of the legendary Great Horned Sea Monster. It is believed that if these scales are exposed during the ritual, the Thunderer and his allies the Thunder-Spirits and the Rain-Spirits, who loathe the Sea Monster, will come with the fury of their storms and clouds and rains to attack their traditional enemy who dares to lift his head out of the stream and to expose a part of his body to the gaze of the Thunder-Beings.

CHRONOLOGY OF THE POEMS

CHRONOLOGY OF THE POEMS

I: TOOTH AND CLAW

To a Wild Goose over Decoys	Begun October, 1914
	Finished 1922
Granite	June, 1923
Four Little Foxes	April, 1923
Feather	July, 1925
Broken Drake	October, 1925
Hang Me Among Your Winds	December, 1923
Feud	Begun September, 1922, Finished 1923
Deep Wet Moss	August, 1924
Angus McGregor	February, 1928
Let Me Go Down to Dust	November, 1924
Frail Beauty	Begun May, 1916, Finished 1919
The World Has a Way with Eyes	May, 1927
To a Grove of Silver Birches	April, 1923
To an Ugly Whelp in a Litter of Wolves	May, 1927
October Gypsy	October, 1928
The Loon	June, 1915
Flame and Smoke	February-March, 1927
Teton Mountain	July, 1921
Wailing Lynx	November, 1925
Blacktail Deer	June, 1923
April Rain	April, 1929
Let Me Flower As I Will	May, 1920
The Wolf Cry	January, 1915
The Granite Mountain	October, 1919
Coyote Brood	April, 1930
Articulate Thrush	June, 1928

Marching Pines	November, 1921
Yellow Moon	February, 1920
Oak	December, 1928
Trailing Arbutus	February, 1920
Fir of the Yule	December, 1927
Winter Oak	January, 1929
Leave Me to My Own	January-March, 1918
Swamp-Owl	September, 1915
Indian Summer	October, 1921
Timber-line Cedar	June, 1921
Bittern	May, 1930
The Great Divide	April, 1915
Philosophic Frogs	December, 1914
Forest Fire	June-October, 1919

XI: FIGURES IN BRONZE

Chief Bloody-Feather, a Council-Chief	June, 1922
Still-Day, the Medicine-Man	August, 1922
Mrs. Down-Stars	March, 1922
Camron, the Indian-Trader	February, 1923
Mr. and Mrs. Peter Big-Cloud	July, 1928
Bazile Dead-Wind, the Beggar	January, 1922
Chief War-Hawk, a Circus Indian	April, 1929
Mrs. Thunder-beater, the Widow	July, 1928
Indian Tryst	June, 1927
The Miscreant, Angel	July, 1922
Teal-Wing, a Council Speaker	December, 1928
Two Chiefs on Parade	August, 1928
Traps-the-Lightning, a Headman	March, 1929

370

INDEX

INDEX OF FIRST LINES

374

375

INDEX OF TITLES

379